12-12-12

LYFE"N"TYME

By

ANGELA RICHARDSON

AKA

AngieSaidThat

Author: Angela Richardson
Prepared for publication: Valerie Perry
Contributor: Kim Hughes
Cover designed by: Newport Prison inmate

Dedications

To the beautiful lyrics of Shekinah Glory Ministry. *"Will your heart and soul say, yes? Will your spirit still say, yes? If I told you what I really need, will your heart and soul say, yes?"*

Valerie Perry, my wife, I can't began to tell you how much I love you and appreciate you. I know it takes a strong minded woman to stand by someone such as myself, AngieSaidThat. This is the name you created and gave to me and it has run you crazy! But, Angie Richardson, love you and thank you for standing by my side. I Love you dearly, *now & later*!

Kim Hughes, hey girl! I want you to know that you really are the greatest even though you can at times be a little devil. GOD places people in our lives for a reason and I thank you so much for the scriptures, positive quotes, and especially for the precious picture of my Mama! Words are not yet found to thank you and I love you!

Tweety, you are really amazing to me. I sometimes wonder why you just don't curse me out in your letters. You have not only been the definition of loyal and friend, you are my angel. I love you!

Shaneika Perry, my step-daughter, I want to thank you so much for believing in me and accepting the love I share with your mother. I will truly bless you through it all. Thanks for typing my movement, my dream series of books. I hope to see that you have written your very own soon too. I love you! "Dad"

Vona Cox, what's your purpose in *Lyfe "N" Tyme*? ...LOL!
Well, I guess you are reading mine all due to a text message I received from you, my long time dear friend. So, is this a Gayle and Oprah thing with us? I pray it becomes one so that I can bless you with the car of your choice. I can't thank you enough for asking me this simply question. *What is your purpose in life?* I love you through it all.

Stanley, Attorney/Pops, I remember our visit at the county jail the day after the judge's birthday when you made the statement, "I can help you work through the system." Well, I did it on my own! You call me the Queen Bee and what did you expect from a "Queen"? Pops, I love you even if you are one of those

3

horses that are out of the barn. My money is always on you! I love you! It's the black in me!

P.S. I'm researching the laws!

Nick, my biological dad, I understand so much now, but it still hurts. I never cared about any of the material things in lyfe "n" tyme. Just a trip to the races meant more to me than anything you ever owned. I never wanted a man like you that had a bunch of women and children, but not enough love or tyme "n" lyfe for any of them. I followed in your footsteps with the women, though. Women of all kind, we don't discriminate! One woman said I got her pregnant, but the test revealed, "I am not the father!" I miss you and I love you! Rest in Peace.

My mother, Elaine Richardson, May 4, 2000, changed my lyfe with no true understanding of my lyfe "n" tyme. You never told me lyfe would be easy. So many days you made it look like a piece of cake and so tasteful. I love you and miss you with every inch of my body, spirit, and soul. I always wanted you to be proud of me and even today mama, "I say yes". I am not by far as strong as you were, but the apple didn't fall too far from the tree. I will never forget the lesson you taught me with *The Purple Hull Peas*. You are my Hero. Rest in Peace.

Psalms 23:6
Surely your goodness and unfailing love will pursue me all the days of my Lyfe.

 I have your charm picture with me now placed in Psalms 32 of the Bible.
The Lord Is Our Shepard!

"Wink!"

Acknowledgments

Shout-out to Dixie Day, JoJo, Lil Red, Bay Bay, Mr. Duely, Lisa Rome, Dot, Rod G., Sweet Tooth, Bop, Ma, Knoxie, Bitty, BeBe, B-Time, E., Bo-Low, Day-One, and many more! We matter buddies and much love!

Sharon, Dollbaby, sister you are the truth! I thank GOD and Mama for giving me the precious gift of having you as my sister. I appreciate all that you have ever done for me in the past, *now & later!* Thank you for sticking by my side during this journey and I love you always more than words could ever express!

To my sisters Marylin, Frenchye, Japan, Debra, Kimberly, Dashunda, Renee, Vernada and Monique. First of all, I love all of you no matter what. To have written the story about LeLe Robertson and her sisters made me feel some type of way. I am truly able to feel her reasons for what she did. I would've been here too if it was one of you guys. It's all about *Lyfe"N"Tyme*. I can't say that would be true if the shoe was on the other foot, the same as LeLe's sisters. But, we both are okay with it on the strength of unconditional love. Love has no limit. I love all of you no matter what through it all. Turn-up the blessings!

Yvette Foster, buddy, my love for you will always remain the same no matter what and I can't wait to come back in your yard. Buddy, I love you, I miss you, and I will soon be back in your yard again and AngieSaidThat!

Mrs. Helen Washington, I know you're okay. I finally understand about death. It's called *Lyfe"N"Tyme*. I love you!

Linda Fitzpatrick, I love and miss you!

Shon Mosley, sista thanks so much for your kind, warm, loving heart and support. Also, tell Lady and Cooper thanks so much. I love you all!

Nicole Broadway, you are spiritually and powerfully in my spirit. I appreciate the love and support.

Karen Coleman, thank you for believing in my vision as an author and understanding the love of writing and thanks to your sister, Martha, who understands the grammatical aspect of it all. It is a blessing to have people such as you two whom GOD has allowed to help with this amazing process.

Dee Dee Newton, you are a very special person with plenty of wisdom and I appreciate you in so many ways and stay prayed up! *Love, Frog*

LeLe Robinson, your *lyfe"n"tyme* is what has made my *tyme* priceless and unregretful as far as my visit to Newport Prison. I am truly remorseful for being a part of any criminal activities. For you to stand before me with such a kind and peaceful spirit on July 16, 2014, with a clip board in hand and asking us in intake what size uniform we needed it seems as your spirit entered mine and till this day has affected my *lyfe"n"tyme*. *S*ista you felt in your heart that you lost your big sister Chris, but since the day I meet you I have called you Baby Girl. You are truly my baby sister. Baby Girl, blood makes you related, but loyalty makes you family. GOD has an impact on our lives and we are truly related through spirit. You are my angel. I love you and you are my hero, *now & later*. Stay prayed up!

PS…I was told you did a praise dance in Wrightsville to the song, *"Yes"*. I will see it for myself once *we* get from behind these white walls. Sista we will praise him in front of many and I love you Baby Girl!

Aleshia Higgins, special shout-out to you girl! Who knew by me meeting your sons…? (Lol) that it would eventually lead to us taking a part of this journey together? GOD truly does place people in a person's life for a reason. You just never know when you are encountering an angel and that's what you are to me! Thank you so much for your research! I sincerely thank you and your husband, George, for the support and love and I love you both! AngieSaidThat

Special thanks to the Newport Prison Officers; Richardson, Branscum, Dewitt, Thayer, Rouse, Jackson, Johnson, Phillips, Nobles, White, Hope, Williams, Canter, Rowlette, Smith, Copper, Ratliff, Whaley and Mallot.

To the women of Newport Prison, many felt my spirit and spoiled me and I truly thank you all. Those that wanted to get to know me on another relationship level, my heart is many miles away from this place, but by all means I'm flattered. I'm trying to do better and I want to be faithful to my wife for a change. This has always been a problem in my *lyfe"n"tyme*. I'm loyal, but faithfulness has a different meaning. This is an example of never to give up on our freedom. In *lyfe"n"tyme* GOD can do the impossible! Let's stay prayed up on the seventy percent law. Our state is truly in need of change. Much love to you all!

To my LGBT community this is for "*The Vine!*"

AngieSaidThat

Words from the Author

Thank you, GOD!

The trouble with lyfe is tyme. We think we have lots of it, but the tyme to start living your lyfe with purpose is TODAY!

I, Angela Richardson, can't express how much I greatly appreciate each reader for supporting such an amazing movement. Most may not believe the spirit, faith, and love that continued to run concurrent in my *Lyfe"N"Tyme*. GOD promised me he would send someone to represent me. And he did it, without a doubt while I'm lying in Barrack 13 on bunk 33 and unknowing what's coming my way.

I want my people to know that if you claim it in Jesus name and believe it, you are going to receive it! I focused and envisioned my series of books touching many people all over, and they will without a doubt! If I didn't believe that I could take the steps to make it happen, there is no way I would've written all these books. This is my fourth book in less than four months of facing an unjust twenty-one year sentence in prison in the State of Arkansas. I can say that GOD created this earth and he's able to move mountains. He can do the impossible. My faith will forever remain in Him, *now & later*.

This has truly been an experience in prison. I don't want to ever mislead my American people and say that people don't deserve imprisonment and there are not evil acts behind these white walls. I once wanted to work inside a prison, but all the money in the world couldn't get me to now, unless the rules regarding fairness and equality change behind these walls. Our system is so quick to punish everyone over one person's behavior. My heart weeps for the beautiful realtor and her family. I lost my sister to Roadie Armstrong and the people in our community thought they knew him. People it's not always someone that's out on parole committing crimes, we all take a chance every day in our *Lyfe"N"Tyme* as we are awakened facing today, tomorrow, and yearly issues.

We have to ask GOD to protect us and our families, as David protected his sheep, but some of us still fear evil. I don't know all the answers, but I do know how to pray and ask for guidance in Jesus name. I've met some great people outside and behind these bars. I have told you the truth and proven facts. There are some things we can't get from commercials, politics, politicians, family, children, preachers, and even some Christians; truth and awareness. I care because we all matter!

This book, *"Lyfe"N"Tyme"*, of my 12-12-12 series will enlighten the community of Little Rock, Arkansas. I'm the first African American lesbian prisoner to ever write a series of books within a year of an unjust hurricane verdict. I'm what many of us give up on and never find, hope and GOD's purpose for our *Lyfe"N"Tyme*. Believe it and receive it in Jesus name!

We as American people must be reminded daily that the devil is real. He's real in these streets and even on a ride to work. Just to be able to share from behind these bars what I read in the daily newspaper and to laugh at the fact that our people need to know there are three sides to every story and the truth usually lies somewhere in the middle. To see Tracy Steele, one of the most powerful men of North Little Rock, resign as the Director of Youth Services lets me know we may never know what a person has witnessed or really goes through in certain positions. Most will look at the fact that his income for this position was over $100,000.00 a year, but some of our people who have a heart, will not allow money to be the reason for hidden evilness.

I see he will resign on October 31st. Halloween! I wonder if *is it a boo or a who with certain people? A trick or a treat?*

True enough he never stated why he resigned and even declined to say what's next in his *lyfe"n"tyme*. Whatever it is, I truly hope on the strength of me knowing this good man from our community, that he finds his purpose with so many choices in his *lyfe"n"tyme*. Shout-out with tons of blessings, Mr. Steele!

It is people like my fellow inmate, Meaka, who needed him around years ago with his involvement in the juvenile justice systems. Someone who related to the youth. I will share Meaka's story later in the book, but my question is, what is a child to do in certain situations when no one really cares?

The state of Arkansas claimed on June 4, 2014, that I, Angela Richardson, was a threat to our community. Not to mention that my great smile which has served more good deeds than those elected during election time caused me an unjust guilty verdict. This is the very same gap in my teeth that has wholeheartedly given to my community. It has also gotten me twenty-one unjust years in prison around an election time. Please allow me to bring to the American people from behind the bars what will be proven facts of my *Lyfe "N" Tyme*!

PS: My buddy, Yvette, told me that this was bigger than me and with GOD all things are possible!

Respectfully submitted,

AngieSaidThat

Introduction

"Somebody loves you, Baby." I tuned into Plies listening to the beginning of the song with the powerful voice of someone we all loved, Patti Labelle. The lyrics of this song took me back to sitting at a desk writing in ink and spilling my heart out. I prayed so much, but I didn't think GOD cared. I prayed for my dear friend, Gayle Woods, whose only son was gunned down by the Maumelle Police Department. No gun was involved. Bryan, only twenty five years old, was shot three times in the chest and twice in the back. Gayle called me during the early morning hours after searching for me on Facebook. She explained to me that GOD had led her to me. She also stated that she continued to pray, but HE kept leading her to me seeking the truth of why she had to watch a video of her only child being gunned down without any understanding or answers.

She took the detective donuts and coffee wanting closure but like the bitter taste of the black coffee, it provided no answers. The sweetness of donuts reminded me of the ones that Donna Faye made at Shipley's Donuts when I was a child. She had worked at Shipley's for years and she always gave me extra donuts. Mama would give us the change from the bottom of her purse every morning to stop by the donut shop on our way to school. The sweet taste of those donuts left special memories that I will never forget. I have no clue as to what Mr. Moe put in those donuts, but the memories of my childhood and the love for certain people are still locked in my heart.

I remember one day as a seventh grader standing in line at the donut shop and seeing my sister, Nana, on her way to Ole Main High School. She was probably in the tenth or eleventh grade. She lived with her first born son, Lil Rod, daddy and grandparents. I really didn't understand it as a child, but now I do. She was young and thought she was in love with Scooby. To this day *"being in love"* has caused many of our teenage

11

girls to leave home at a young age and become young mothers. We must find ways to address situations such as these and have better communication within our schools versus punishment all the time.

After seeing my sister, I didn't want the donuts anymore. I wanted her to enjoy them, so I placed my quarters in her hand and never told mama.

Today, now with her first born in prison, it seems as if a part of my sister has died. Because Lil' Rod didn't understand the law, it cost him to serve unjust time. My friend, Denise's baby boy at the age of fifteen was offered a cigarette and a cheeseburger by a detective and it also caused him to serve unjust time.

Many Americans burn their gas rushing to the polls to vote because of what the candidates have promised them just to win their votes at election time. To pick up the newspaper and see that one of our politicians in Washington, D.C., who has served fairly for many years and believed in justice, was retiring this year brought several questions to mind. Who can we turn to now? It's a very low chance that the District of Washington D.C., will ever hear about our natural state again. Hear our cries for justice. It's not just in the state of Arkansas either, it's everywhere. Will we ever again have one man to care about the jobs of so many citizens? How can we help get those who care about some of the American people to care the same about all people and not only those who are able to vote? To love everybody as GOD loves us. Equally! The prosecutors have a job to do, that's understandable, but do they offer everyone fair plea deals?

What I love about this book the most is that my readers will feel every beat of my heart. GOD said in Psalms 58, *"Practice justice not violence"*. I'm not a threat to our society and I wouldn't hurt a fly. I'm a blessing *now & later* and I am free from the addiction of gambling.

Much love and bountiful blessings to us all in Jesus name.

Angie Richardson

VS

The State of Arkansas

Chapter 1

D.R. Court, Ugh! ...What is One to Do?

Today, after chow I stood in line waiting to finally talk to the Major. I couldn't get my experience on Friday off my mind. I got my first D.R. (Disciplinary Report) write-up and prison court punishment. It was the weekend and most people are excited about no school. Some of us had ordered Inmate Counsel Food, but this time I really couldn't enjoy my salad. Later that morning around 8:30 AM the officer shouted, "Disciplinary Court!"

I got in line to walk down to the central station as a group of officers stood there waiting on the pineapple prisoners to check-in and take a seat. Jemeaka smiled the entire time. She really didn't care about any of it, but I certainly felt some type of way. I looked over at A.B., who has served 18 years and knew very well that I wasn't supposed to have those stationery items, even though I needed them to mail off my Rule 37 Appeal. Commissary had been out of the large envelopes for two weeks. I wasn't mad at A.B., because I understand women will go the extra mile if they want to get your attention. It was just another example of an irritating learning experience for me again not knowing. Very much like the learning experience of my trial on June 3 & 4, 2014.

I was angry more at myself than at A.B., and what pissed me off is that the staff is quick to tell you what's written in the handbook. It reminds me of the Pulaski County Jail at 3201 W. Roosevelt, where the rules are subject to change at any time of the day. It's okay for the staff to go against the rules, but as a prisoner and not of the right skin color, having same-sex preferences, and not being one of the Major's favorites, it's a different story.

You are simply a nobody! Especially if your family doesn't call out of concern for you. That's pretty much what we are in Newport Prison. Meaningless! Nobody cares what happens to us behind these bars.

I sat in the chair listening to Jemeaka talk and watching her do the hand signs of the prison language. She is so good at it and I wonder if there is a sign language class offered here. My stomach suddenly became weakened and I wanted to vomit as my name was called.

"Richardson!" Sgt. Martinez called.

Sgt. Martinez is white, 5'9", 285 lbs., glasses, and has big hands and feet.

"Turn around, face the wall, and place your hands behind your back." He demanded.

Sgt. Martinez placed the handcuffs on my wrists. He and his wife, Mrs. Martinez, are over the safety meetings on Friday mornings.

He took me by my arm and escorted me inside a room (a warden named Mr. Burks). He is a pale white man, 5'8", 215 lbs., sandy hair, glasses, wearing a purple shirt, black tie, and black slacks.

I sat in a visitation chair looking at a T.V. monitor facing the prison judge, Mr. Kenneth Water. He has black hair, dark skin, as if he was mixed with Indian or Mexican genes.

"Ms. Richardson, do you understand your charges here today?" He asked.

"No Sir, I do not." I answered.

"ADC (Arkansas Department of Corrections) disciplinary hearing action code violations; 12-1: Failure to obey verbal and /or written order of staff. 15-1: The purchase or exchange of unauthorized articles or of unauthorized articles through unauthorized channels on 09/11/2014 @ 2:40 PM."

As he read off the paperwork, I could barely hear over the officer's radio.

"So, how do you plead?" He asked.

"Not guilty, Sir." I answered.

"Well, I will give you a chance to explain yourself." He replied.

"Sir, this is my first time in prison and I wasn't aware that this inmate of 18 years wasn't allowed to give me envelopes and folders to mail off my legal work. I was in the intake area for almost two months and I do apologize, Sir." I explained.

"I find you guilty and order you to serve 20 days without commissary. No phone for 20 days. No visitation for 20 days. And your class reduced to Class Three. You have the right to appeal this case." He stated.

Sgt. Martinez marched me back out in handcuffs and another female officer asked.

"Is she going to the hole?"

Another officer even got on the radio and said.

"I need a bed for another prisoner for the hole."

I instantly started sweating and was somewhat puzzled.

Sgt. Martinez stepped in and said.

"No, take the cuffs off of Richardson. She's free to return back to her Barrack." He stated smiling.

I felt some type of way after I got out of those handcuffs. My mind raced repeatedly over this date, 9/19/2014 @ 10:40 – 10:45 AM. This hearing took place the same way as my short two day trial on June 3rd & 4th, which left me facing twenty-one years of unjust time for not knowing. Who really cares?

To be honest, its prisoners like Jemeaka, who intentionally go to the hole for cursing out the staff just to be with their girlfriends. I didn't understand yet that it was people in here who cut themselves or exchanged pills for commissary items and got dropped to a minor, but were able to keep their class. But, I'm just another black prisoner in a white uniform. They are very prejudiced against interracial couples and most black studs catch hell in here.

I walked back to Barrack 16 really in my feelings about all of it. I felt helpless, but my faith wouldn't allow me to let them get the best of me. I must admit that in less than one short week, the inmates in Barrack 16 had really gotten attached to me. I really felt a lot of peace and great spirits around me. I was able to focus without any distractions.

Again, the devil has his way of trying to control someone. He hates the fact I'm no longer one of his team players, *now & later*! GOD allows me to be aware of my surroundings, and HE knew overall that I didn't want to be placed in the pits of this prison. I've been told you can only shower three times a week and your mat is taken in the early AM hours of the morning. No commissary and a mess within itself in the hole!

8:30 PM

"Richardson, pack up. You're moving!" The officer yelled.

I prayed about it and asked GOD to just stand by me. I'm a true soldier at heart, but this was trying to get the best of me. I see why so many prisoners are held back in prison and easily denied parole. Now that I'm here, I'm finally able to enlighten the public. I have to wait sixty days to get my Class 2 back and then an additional thirty days to receive my Class 1 back in order to move back into Housing Unit Three. I'm unsure of what Barrack 16 holds!

When I was told to pack up, inmates Wendy and Mrs. Dawson came over to my bunk. They couldn't hold back their tears. An inmate name Kenya held Mrs. Dawson as tears fell from her eyes. Another inmate name DeeDee helped me pack. Again, same as the last move, I pulled out the pictures of me to remind them of the laughter and overall of the most unforgettable person name AngieSaidThat!

I couldn't thank GOD enough for allowing the very same elderly woman who stopped by earlier from The Pals Program to lay praying hands on my book. The very same woman from Heber Springs, Arkansas, who prayed for the ending of *"12-12-12 The Cries Behind The Bars"* in Unit 19. GOD truly has His way and I thank Him.

As I packed I knew I would miss them. Moving out of Barrack 16 made me feel some type of way. Now sitting in Housing 2, Barrack 13, on bunk 33, I felt sad after coming back from the Major's office trying to get some type of prison understanding. I left her office feeling even worse than my experience in prison court.

She sat at her desk looking at me as I explained. "Major, I would like to talk to you about my write-up. This is my first time in prison. I'm no trouble and I need to understand our rights as a prisoner." The time was 11:33 AM on 9/22/2014.

"Well, tell me what you have to say and what happened in court." She said.

"I was in intake for almost two months and with no phone calls for exactly two months before approval. Now I'm on a twenty day restriction for not knowing that inmate A.B. couldn't give me stationary. Commissary didn't have any in stock and I was simply trying to mail my appeals out. Warden Frances told me it would be a minor and it wasn't. Now, I'm busted on my class already and on a twenty day restriction. Major, I owned the only black gay club in Little Rock and I know how to avoid women who are attracted to me." I stated.

"You owned what?" She asked looking over her glasses the same way Judge Judy looked over hers.

"A black gay club." I replied as Warden Frances and Warden Burkes, a male warden, walked into the Major's office and joined the conversation.

"So, what do you want me to do?" The Major asked.

"I'm asking for my class back." I answered.

"You have already been to court and it's nothing I can do about it." She stated.

What she didn't know is that I knew on September 20, 2014, Missy, a white inmate with numerous write-ups, had gotten a written disciplinary from the same officer that drilled me over having some ice. "Retch Now, Mr. Gupie!" reminded me of my old high school coach, Randy, from Ole Main High School. But their ways and personality were totally different. This officer seemed mad at the world and he hated his job. As a prisoner, I've learned to speak with respect. "Sir, how is your day? Enjoy your weekend. Thank you! Thanks a lot!" ...and so on, but

19

its officers like him behind these prison walls that hate life and hate people.

The Major repeated to Warden Frances what I shared with her about it being a major write-up versus a minor write-up.

"I want to think that you are smarter than that, saying you didn't know." She stated as she pulled her long hair trying to pin it up. "No, I didn't tell her it would be a minor. She didn't want to tell me who gave the items to her. I had to tell her she would go to the hole and that it was stealing. She has the right to appeal it and my youngest daughter knows not to take anything that doesn't belong to her. That's being ignorant." She said pulling her black hair up into a bun and placing a hair clip on it while looking at me.

"Warden Frances, can I say something?" I asked.

"Yes." She answered.

"I'm smart and not knowing doesn't make me ignorant and it will not happen again. Y'all have a nice day." I said as I got up and walked out really feeling some type of way. The fact of her comparing me to her youngest daughter, calling me ignorant, and saying that I was not being smart was too much. I thought to myself, she must not know about me as T.I.'s voice played in my head. *"U Don't Know Me."* But, of course I'm not one of the Major's favorites, like Missy. But, people never know who's representing GOD's work. Even in prison Joseph, Paul, Silas, and Timothy may not have walked behind Newport Prison's yellow line, but people should be careful how they treat his people who have discovered their purpose in *lyfe"n"tyme*, even in an all white uniform behind these prison walls. People do not allow the fabric of your clothing to have you thinking your better than one of GOD's children. He meant love us as He loves you. He has his way of revealing the sheep in wolves clothing.

I returned to Barrack 13 to all the noise and drama. My new top bunkmate in bunk 34 name Missy, has more energy than the energizing bunny. Missy is white, 5'4", 120 lbs., brownish hair and grey eyes. She enjoys hustling pills. I will later share her story as a meth cooker, her addiction, and ending the life of her husband in Fayetteville, Arkansas.

Returning back in my feelings about the Major and Warden Frances. I plugged my ears with Missy's MP4 player and listened to *"Blame It on Me"* by Chrisette Michelle. *"You can say whatever you like. Blame it on me. Say it's my fault. I really don't care."*

I placed the song on repeat and my ink spilled my feelings onto paper the same as the tears that rolled down my face last night. While others whispered late at night, snored, and farted different smells, I decided to listen to one of the greatest and most unforgettable voices that most people dream of having, Ms. Whitney Houston. *"Where Do Broken Hearts Go?"* What happened on this day didn't cause any tears, actually it allowed me to write and share my thoughts. Whitney's song took me outside of this gated community with the thoughts of my family, relationships, and past experiences. Again, T.I., made it clear. *"What all don't kill you, will make you stronger"* from the song *"Motivation"*.

`\   Even though I'm now placed on restriction, I had enough food to snack on and I had my way of getting what I wanted. As long as you're a stud, it's possible. Most studs have come to prison knowing that the women will entertain them. To be good looking will have many women tricking off their commissary. Most headhunters know that it's different outside these walls. The attention inside prison is totally different.

Now, I've been told that a stud by the name of Hershey claims she pulled a gun on me and couldn't wait until I arrived because she was going to check me. Most would say it's going down on site, meaning no words exchanged and I got you nigga, we going nite-nite!

21

King Avenue made it her business to relay the message the same as she did today in the chow-hall about A.B. talking about me admitting that she gave me those items.

I looked up at her and told her I cared not to hear it. I could care less who has anything to say inside or outside of these walls. Why is she mad? I mean to be honest, as I share with my readers, A.B. is a cool person and I pray after 18 years of this prison life she finds her purpose in *lyfe"n" tyme*. As far as the stud, Hershey who is 5'5", 150 lbs., chocolate, gold teeth, once wore dreads but now has a low haircut, and can't talk a lick. I have very well seen her plenty of times at my events and I have never had a problem with her. She has a bad drug addiction, but we all have something in life wrong with us. The first time we saw one another behind these bars we spoke.

"What's up Bro, you good?" She asked.

"Yeah, yeah!" I answered. I have nothing against anybody. I'm past it and I'm sure of who I am.

We both had contact with a certain female a long time ago, but I'm way past that. I never made the female my lady due to the fact that she had no clue as to how to tell the truth of *"lyfe"n"tyme"* nor how to be a woman. She lied more than the law allowed and I guess Hershey fell in love with her looks and most surely her lies.

Now, if it makes some stud's day to say that we beefing over an ex-lover or even someone I've had connections with, at the end of the day they're still not AngieSaidThat. I'm unforgettable in everyone's heart and *lyfe*. All I can tell you is to tune in and listen to *"How to Hate"* by Lil Wayne & T-Payne.

I was instantly reminded of some of the drama at my club, Club Goodtimes @ 3910 Asher Avenue, by the gossip, the relationship drama, and the gay families of King Avenue and Snap straight beefing over some of the female pineapple prisoners. Two studs that's been friends or at least they claimed to be, like most studs do, but end up sleeping with the same girls. The same way I kept my distance from most outside these white walls, it's nothing different in prison. I acknowledge my own kind, but again, the chocolates (my niggas) are the main ones that are afraid to stand together or up for anything. We need to enjoy one another and try sticking together like the whites, Latinos, and Mexican people are in unity.

I've realized for a fact that this prison is a big playground for homosexuals. The policies and procedures will never make any progress or anything else as far as trying to solve the gay relationship problems and behaviors. In order to be with that special one they have fallen in love with or head over hills for, some inmates are cutters, some fight on purpose, and some think of other ways to go to the hole with their mates. The behavior guideline issues are in need of a major change. To look around this prison and listen to John Legend's, *"All of Me"*, so many of the prisoners feel every lyric of this song. People have to realize we are not any different than judges, preachers, attorneys, or others simply wanting to enjoy *"lyfe "n" tyme"* with that special person. Is it fair that we should be placed in the pits of this prison and punished over what we feel in our hearts and those we love?

I've seen the sex in the shower, on the back of the toilet, and have sat up in my bunk and listened to it. I've been told that throughout the years a lot has changed with the kitchen sex action on the beans and rice. It is not just here in Newport Prison. People are going to have sex. It's certain things I do and do not agree with behind these white wall. I have ideas that can help a lot in this prison in spite of Warden Frances calling me ignorant and saying that even her youngest daughter is smarter than I am. A lot of people are quick to put their children on a pedestal, but the devil also attacks children. And it don't matter whose child it is in his eyes. I look at her totally different now. I found myself attracted to the warden until today. In a split second, my mind and spirit were no longer overtaken by the beauty of flesh and a smile.

Before my imprisonment my buddy, Yvette, spoke so highly of her. Now, I just know to stay out of her way. For those who judge our homosexual lifestyle and relationships, you too will be judged. Regardless of a person's position or beliefs, we are human too! It's happening every day. The people thought of as "going to get paid regardless" are having sex. *Regardless*, I love myself and I am able to deal with the inmates in a totally different way. People should learn how to appreciate the love of Christ. I've watched these inmates with cancer trade their medicine for commissary, which is a major D.R., but some of the inmates are so cool with most of the officers that it is almost as if I'm on the outside of this prison watching the hook-ups go down. And as you know and please always remember, it's not what ya' know, it's who ya' know at all times. It's called *Lyfe "N" Tyme*!

Chapter 2

"I Just Have Good Hair"

Yesterday a young lady across the hall in Barrack 14 got locked up in the hole for putting fingernails, toe nails, and boo-boo on noodles and eating it. This is the same prisoner who jacked off with a baby powder bottle. She's currently in the hole, but some of these write-ups never make it to the office at Pine Bluff, Arkansas.

If the staff would've been paying more attention to the Chaplain program versus the homosexuals, there is no telling what type of money could've been saved. I have never known an inmate to get out and get a home built, a new car, and money from the great Christian programs through grant funding and Inmate Counsel fundraising. What about the profits from the photos taken on Sundays? So much dirt is going on behind these walls.

I was even told SNAP, food stamps benefits, are provided for each prisoner, but four to five times a week the same ole so-called beef is served with five different names. And what about the online internet lies and false written documentation to get grant funding?

Does anyone know or care about the unhealthy and unsanitized usage of the water lines for the sewage, the showers, the kitchen, and the drinking water that are all connected to one pipe line? And this prison uses its own private company to do inspections in order to pass the inspections. Last week one of the air conditioner units caught fire in Barrack 8. Was that reported on the news?

I've asked the studs to write about the mistreatment and racism against us. But they are all afraid of going to the hole or other actions being taken against them. Well, I decided to follow all the rules stated in the outdated handbook and continue my purpose with my *lyfe"n"tyme*. GOD knows once he opens these doors and remove these prison chains, it's no looking back for AngieSaidThat!

It is a fact that a lot of parolees return to prison after only being released for six months. Last year a black man in Little Rock got out and killed someone from a well-known family and now all the rules apply to the people out on parole. This is why the system needs to be changed and upgraded. Not all prisoners, parolees, judges, attorneys, and teachers should be punished over someone else's actions. Stanley doesn't think I know he has dealings with those horses that he told me about. He told me that all the horses were out of the barn, but what he failed to realize is that I love him in spite of it all. We all make decisions in our *life"n"tyme*. Good and bad! AngieSaidThat

As the clock struck 4:00 PM, some of the inmates walked in from both work and school. I was tuned into Justin Timberlake and Beyoncé's, *"Until the End of Time"* and had made the decision not to join the others going to the chow-hall. To be honest I really didn't want to see Warden Frances in the hallway or take the chance of a petty write-up. I found out earlier that the menu consisted of turkey bologna, mashed potato, crushed pineapples, and squash. I'm sure the "beef" is somewhere waiting to be served! Yesterday we had the privilege of enjoying some chicken pot pie, which I very well enjoyed.

A black officer, name Sgt. Ox, who 5'7", 175 lbs., glasses, hair slick back in an old fashion bun and country as all get out, looked at my hair and said.

"Look, you're not going to be able to come out the Barrack with dreads or twists in your hair!"

She placed fear in my heart. OMG, I'm thinking David Bro, protect your sheep and this blonde curly hair of mine!

"Sgt. Ox, this is my hair. It's naturally curly and I just have good hair." I replied showing her the roots of the black new growth of my hair.

"Look, don't try it with me! I'm black just like you and you better take those twists out of your hair before I write up a major disciplinary!" She stated, looking like Dee from the T.V. series *"What's Happening?"*

"Yes, Sgt. Ox." I said and walked off.

I went inside Barrack 13 and put some oil in my hair which only made it shine and the curls look even better. What is one to do? The thought of her telling me she's black and knows black people hair really made me feel some type of way.

I picked up the phone to call my wife, praying they had not restricted my calls yet. This was too much after prison court and now this mess over a black officer not even having enough hair to be brushed back, much less know the different textures of all black hair. She looked like she had about two pieces of dental floss holding her hair together and brushed to the back, not to mention Sgt. Ox's hair is short enough to roll with rice and use one commissary Fruit Loop cereal for the ponytail holder. Ugh!

"Valerie, baby, look this is enough with me this week." I said. "How are you doing, Baby? I asked after I got my first sentence out.

"Baby, I'm doing fine. What's wrong with you?" She asked.

"Baby, I already told you about the envelopes and prison court. I hate this petty mess, and now a black officer told me that she's going to write me up about my hair, thinking I'm trying to grow dreads or twist. I told her it was my texture of hair. Plus last week another white officer asked me how did my hair turn blonde? She thought I had used the chemicals that the prisoners use for their dentures and that's a major write-up. I had to show her my I.D. to prove I came here with blonde curly hair." I explained and she knew I was pissed listening to my heart of frustrations and truths.

"Are you for real? Baby, look I'm going to e-mail Warden Frances and I'm going to call LaShay. She will be the one to get them told. LaShay don't play!" She stated.

"Baby, yes call her and tell her all I've told you. LaShay worked at the Pulaski County Jail for over ten years and knows how they are. She hates that place now. But, I can bear what's being thrown my way here. I hold my tongue, but these people will try and break a person down. It's never their fault, Baby, they always justify their actions and I'm sick of it. Y'all need to let them know there are people out there who love me in this *lyfe"n"tyme* the same as their folks love them. I stated and we continued talking about more positive things.

Hours later it was mail call at 7:30 PM. I only got one piece of paper, my tyme card. I tore it up and placed in the trash. It wasn't a part of my lyfe nor the correct tyme. As the other inmates read their mail, I watched T.V. and made bowls of prison meals to eat. I laid down and took a nap feeling some type of way. I tuned out the noise and just wanted to sleep. I wanted my friend, Likita Rucker, to come back into my dreams and I didn't want to wake up to the reality of imprisonment. Receiving mail and being able to make phone calls makes serving prison time easier to deal with in *lyfe"n"tyme*. Those of you that claim to miss me who have access to the internet can look up my contact information by simply logging onto the ADC Inmate Search to contact me here in prison ...Hmmm!

Around 9:00 PM, I woke up to the noise of everybody taking showers, laughing and talking. I got up to shower and put my state issued uniform in the laundry. The one thing this prison did do on a daily basis was the laundry! In Barrack 16, I was a laundry porter, we passed out the laundry every day, but in my favor the women would let me write and never disturbed me about helping them with the laundry. But, I would do my duties at later times due to certain officers like Sgt. Ox watching me.

Last night I pulled my mat up to position it as if it was on a sofa to write until the AM hours. I plugged Missy's MP4 ear plugs into my ears and she insisted I listen to songs off the playlist that she made especially for me. Kelly Rowland's *"Every Time You Walk out That Door"* was the truth. Honestly it was the first time I had heard it and I loved it. It's amazing how music can take you there and I'm not referring to the races. It takes me outside of these prison walls.

Every day we look at the lay-in sheet, a sheet that schedules and tracks the prisoner's daily movement. My name was listed on 9/23/2014 at 8:30 AM for the Law Library until 9:30 AM. I was also scheduled for 3:40 PM to 3:45 PM for a dental hygiene appointment. I picked up the phone wanting to call my wife, but my restriction wouldn't allow my call to go through.

I later found out Safari was placed back in the hole for fighting her ex- lover. It had me all in my feelings. I know for a fact that if I was in the Barrack with her this would have been avoided. I have written a request and asked Warden Frances to allow me to be a mentor to her. But, no one listens. This is my point, that certain actions and behaviors could be avoided with our troubled LGBT youth behaviors.

To be called ignorant or not smarter than her youngest daughter was an insult when I knew my ideas could change and improve the conditions inside of these prison walls. I have expertise. I have lived it, walked it, and created it. Surely, it doesn't take an education to create useful ideas that can bring about changes for the betterment of everyone. Anybody can go to school and follow assignments and get to be in authority, but can those people solve the problems of today's issues. I don't think so! In fact, even in this prison, records will show that I'm not lying, not one person ever would've thought that a black, gay, ignorant with the mindset of a child would be in all white as a prisoner writing long hours about the *lyfe"n"tyme* of prisoners, staff, and the State of Arkansas.

One thing I know is that I would like for the state of Arkansas to acknowledge that I never received the recognition in my community for my good deeds or accomplishments from the city nor the state. But when a person such as myself decide to try GOD and not give up on my purpose in *lyfe"n"tyme* and realize through Christ that all things are possible! It's much easier to give up, but not AngieSaidThat!

I very well remember as a child my mama had us picking and peeling purple hull peas. She had us pick out the rotten ones and place the good ones in a big bowl. Mama would wash and cook them with other delicious foods to make a great meal. Just like the peas, I know we have good politicians, preachers, attorneys, parents, children, mechanics, school teachers and etc., and I know we have rotten ones too. I've looked around this prison and we have our good officers, prisoners, and staff, and rotten ones as well. As I continued to write I listened to the lyrics, *"If Somebody Loves You, Will They Always Love You, Where Do Broken Hearts Go?" and "I've been around and around enough to Know That Dreams Don't Turn to Gold".* I love Whitney Houston. The music from the soul is the truth and lets us all stay connected. My mama had us in training by being so young and picking purple hull peas and separating the rotten ones from the good ones without even understanding what *lyfe"n"tyme* had in store for us. It was food to our hearts and soul.

Chapter 3

Monique Sharpen

12:00 AM

My mind thought about inmate, Monique Sharpen. I looked over to the left, one bunk over from me and she was covered in all white with a towel over her eyes to block out the lights. As the guard made her hourly rounds, Moe asked me to help her write a reconsideration letter. She was trying to go back before the parole board after receiving a one year denial for her charges of first degree battery, forgery, theft of property, breaking and entering, and one other charge from July 1, 2014.

Her inmate timecard read theft of property, forgery, probation revocation 2006, breaking and entering, and habitual offender 2013. Time served in jail 439 days. I advised her of her rights after carefully reading her affidavit of what they claim as facts and evidence alleging probable cause. Monique's case really puzzled me and not to mention she thought her grandmother had hired a good attorney to represent her case.

Monique's grandmother, til this day wants to find the man that impersonated being an attorney. My question is how is it that he was so easily able to visit these clients in the county jail. This never made the big bold black print in the newspaper or on the news. Is it all about *lyfe"n"tyme?* I have advised Monique from my studies in the Law Library that I will surely assist her with writing a letter to the parole board for reconsideration of her one year denial. She served 439 days on a charge she didn't ever get served a warrant on. Later the charges changed. Wow! Our American voters would be surprised by the truth of some issues behind these prison walls and paperwork.

People what should we do about lies and hidden evidence? What about those that throw the rock and hide their hand? We all at some point believe in those who claim they want to help us. Even the Chaplin here at Newport Prison for many years, who used GOD's words, is scandalous. The Chaplin returned from a trip to Haiti talking about how he wanted to help them build a church and give to the indigent, the same as the inmate church program in this prison. I really felt his spirit the very first Sunday I saw him. Rumors were already in our hood about his involvement with an inmate that served ten years behind these bars. Is it true that sex will get you freedom and certain positions in *lyfe"n"tyme*?

What about the *lyfe"n"tyme* of school teachers and administration workers in Lonoke, North Little Rock, and at Little Rock schools like St. Mary's and Mill's High School? The teachers in authority are involved with students and most claim the students freely teach them the 69 position. Let's solve this problem today, no math needed lawmakers!

Inmate Stephanie is tall, 5'8", 155 lbs., beautiful black hair, big pretty brown eyes, dimples, thin narrow lips, thin nose and attractive. I remember as a child my junior high school teachers, Miss Kissinger, Ms. Amy, and Sharon Serio. I wanted to take them apples from the Food King store and not one time thinking about sex. I also enjoyed the Young Life Organization with Norman and his wife, Ann. I thought Melinda and Christy were two very attractive women, but not one time did I think of sex. My dear friends, Andrea Rodger and Andrea Jenkins, were drop dead gorgeous, but never thinking sex. I truly had some very attractive friends, but I never thought of sex with any of them.

I now wonder if our coach, who is married to a high school friend of mine, ever propositioned her. A left handed basketball player making plenty of free throw shots back in the late 80's at Ole Main High School. I mean we were all "Wildcats", but I know for a fact that she was a virgin. Today they are still married with beautiful children and I love them through it all.

These are my thoughts at 2:00 AM while writing and listening to *"The Only One"* by Evanescence. Go Wildcats! Angiesaidthat

Chapter 4

The Law Library

I can very well vision Andrea Rogers reading my series of books and laughing. It's all about *lyfe"n"tyme*. The song *"Unapologetic"* is now playing by Rihanna. As a prisoner, I'm still able to keep my heart open even though the state of Arkansas claims to own me on this date of September 23, 2014. *"It Ain't the Whiskey"* by Gary Allan played next on Missy's MP4 player.

A little while later Missy's voice from the top bunk wakes me.

"Angie, get off the blanket and let me cover you up with my robe." She demanded.

My top bunkmate, Missy has so much energy. It's so cold that I covered up with every state provided item I possibly could. Others laughed at me to see me in thermals, a robe, and the winter jacket under both blankets as I sipped on hot tea to remain warm while writing.

I didn't even hear the officer yell chow-time or anything else. I have been told there are four or five stages of sleep. I drifted off in the deepest stage after writing until the early AM hours and listening to great music that I felt within my body and soul.

7:30 AM

"Angie, get up for your appointment." It was Missy's voice again. Every day I would lie quietly praying and asking GOD to guide me through another day behind these bars. I got up and used the restroom, brushed my teeth, and washed my face. Missy was putting on her makeup listening to her MP4 player and singing loudly. I slipped on my state issued shirt and pants looking forward to my favorite part of this prison experience, the law library and my appointment with Mrs. Robbins. I mistakenly thought it was at 8:30 AM this morning. I rechecked the lay-in sheet and clearly it said 8:00 AM. I rushed to get my paperwork together and to get ready for the day in my *lyfe"n"tyme* behind the bars of Newport Prison.

After my one hour of studying and quickly writing notes to advise and write a reconsideration letter for Monique, I packed up for my next stop. At count time I got stuck waiting in the hallway to see Mrs. Robbins. In the midst of waiting at Barrack 13 for my 9:25 AM appointment others shopped commissary.

Missy, who has an OPA, (an out of place assignment disciplinary), and a talking in the hall disciplinary, disappeared even though her name appeared on the layout sheet for court. After Saturday's visit with the major, the following week I requested to speak with Mrs. Robbins. This is what I call *lyfe"n"tyme* at Newport Prison. I walked into Mrs. Robbins office and signed in on September 23, 2014 at 10:32 AM. She's always dressed to impress. Mrs. Robbins is black, nice texture of short hair, and nice stylish glasses. She had on a red blouse, black slacks, silver stone accessories, and a pair of black shoes, and a nice stone ring on her left finger.

"Hello, Mrs. Robbins." As I spoke, I noticed the white woman that sits across from her had on a shirt with a collar with ADC printed on it.

"Hello, so you need an envelope to mail off your Rule 37?" She asked.

"Yes." I answered smiling.

"I have to give you two of them and send one to the judge, the court clerk, and the prosecutor." She said.

"So, I can place two copies inside the one to the clerk and the judge?" I asked.

"Yes." She answered.

"Mrs. Robbins, I want to thank you for helping me. You will understand a lot later." I stated.

"You're welcome." She replied smiling.

She picked up the telephone to answer a call and I tuned in without her having knowledge of me listening to her conversation as she smiled while talking.

"Yes, add dressing in the slaw while making it. Well, the anniversary is tomorrow and I got a wreath made in orange and black.   I hope Randall has it hung up by the time I get home." She giggled talking on the phone with a stack of request forms in her hand fanning herself. "I love you too." She ended the conversation and looked over at me and said. "I get hot flashes." We all laughed.

Jill, her prisoner assistant, has been very helpful to all of the prisoners wanting to study the law and helped in any way possible. She was sweet and kind. I told her about my write-up and she advised me to stay out of trouble and told me it was called trafficking and trading by taking things from another inmate. I got my legal mail and signed out her office to return back to my Barrack.

I walked down the hall back to Barrack 13 really feeling good about using my time wisely and quickly getting notes to hopefully be able to help write Monique's reconsideration letter. I returned back to see Missy with a bag of commissary and exchanging some for pills.

I asked her. "Missy, how do you get those items to your pill connection?"

"Well, Stephanie and I both do it either during chow or pill call. You will be surprised at how much we get away with in here." she bragged.

"Well, if you're white, you're right. If you're light, you might. But if you black, get the hell back!" I said smiling and telling the truth and we all laughed.

Missy stated. "Well, the Major don't want me with a black stud. She told me its trouble. They make sure that Safari and I stay separated because of our history. To be honest, it's always the black studs fault in the staff eyes and I'm an angel in the major's eyes." She explained smiling.

Speaking of the devil, I looked up as the major walked in Barrack 13 at 1:00 PM. She looked around being very observant, but had no clue of me watching her twice as closely and taking notes as she talked briefly with some of her favorite inmates until Missy walked over to her. They talked and giggled for a short time. She didn't have any knowledge of me being observant around her compound.

Another prisoner, Keisha, who was on the top bunk to the right of me said.

"Don't y'all get quiet now! Don't stop talking because the major is in here."

The Major is 5'5", 230 lbs., short blonde hair, glasses and never smiles unless it's for her favorite people. She had no idea of my thoughts as I watched her. I tried to show her just a few hours ago a few pictures of my LGBT movements and share ideas they might want to consider in this prison while I was standing and waiting for Mrs. Robbins. But, again, I'm too ignorant with the mindset of the warden's youngest daughter. Who would actually listen to a black soft stud with blonde hair and dressed in all white in Newport Prison? Nobody, but GOD!

Later, I picked up an old newspaper dated, September 21, 2014, and understood why Newport, Arkansas, was in need of change.

Newport was looking to attract graduates in a bid to stop "Brain Drain". For years Newport, along with most small Arkansas towns have seen youngsters leave the area to attend college in a bigger town and never return. The business experts referred to it as "Brain Drain". Rather than losing people to migration they want to attract them back to the town on the banks of the White River. We have youths in Little Rock who move to bigger cities and never come back as well. Newport hopes that eventually they will move back, however, this city is so far behind on what's important to the youth.

Many will find themselves in Little Rock living as if they were in New York City once they leave Newport. The students of Little Rock who have studied and experienced UALR, UAPB, Philander Smith College, Arkansas Baptist, or Shorter College will move to bigger cities such as Dallas, Atlanta, Chicago, or move to states like Florida or North Carolina, which are more prosperous states, especially for blacks. Once they leave the state they will by all means find themselves only visiting what they use to call home. The paper stated that Newport is now a dying town and the residents state that something must be done. My advice is to turn Newport into a retirement community. People are too busy judging others and stuck on outdated issues. It is time for a change in Newport, Arkansas" Brain Drain"!

At this time of unknowing who our new elected politicians will be and to be reading the newspaper trying to stay connected with the spirit of my community's needs, I'm very concerned about my troubled LBGT youth. I've witnessed a lot inside this prison on a daily basis and we are in trouble due to same-sex issues. Our leaders are quick to mislead the public, but I'm here behind the bars to enlighten the public with the thoughts of just thinking about what if it was their very own child. We all know that education is one of the major issues at election time. We all need to learn how to keep it real at elections in our *lyfe"n"tyme!*

Chapter 5

Politicians and Their Politics

Sunday, September 21, 2014

The B Section in the Arkansas Democrat Gazette newspaper reports that Governor Beebe papers and furniture are going to ASU. Governor Mike Beebe announced Saturday that he plans to donate his gubernatorial papers to Arkansas State University, where they will be archived and held in the vacant historic V. C. Kays House on the Jonesboro campus. Beebe has already donated to the University his papers from when he was Attorney General from 1983 - 2003.

He stated. "I've made no secret of my love for Arkansas State University. I've been fortunate to participate in many historic Arkansas events during my 32 years."

Also, former Governor Mike Huckabee's papers are at Ouachita Baptist University in Arkadelphia. Five past governors papers including those of Winthrop and Bumpers are housed at the University of Arkansas at Little Rock and Bill Clinton's is at the Central Arkansas Library Butler Center.

Well, it makes me wonder, whose papers are donated to our black colleges such as Arkansas Baptist, Philander Smith College, and Shorter College. Don't let me leave out UAPB. Maybe my buddies, Nette Davis, Vona Cox, Robbie Brooks, and J. Love papers are at UAPB with historic value. What is the reason as to why I helped my black gay community for over 13 years, but was never acknowledged for any of it? I've given more than papers and furniture. I've paid for burial services for AIDS/HIV victims, but does it even matter? To all the governors listed above, my papers will make a black history series of books. The AngieSaidThat series!

Again, politics remind me so much of Facebook and commercials. Most are able to hide behind a camera and be whoever they want to be. Due to the fact I love certain people who are friends with most of the elected politicians, I will not ever write about what I very well can prove. I'm not afraid of the fact that it might cost my life to be taken. My freedom has been unfairly taken on sentencing by the state. I could very well write another true story that will raise a lot of controversy, but it's not about getting back at any one. It's not going to ease my pain. I'm doing whatever I need to do in order to make sure that nobody in our diverse community and troubled LGBT community ever feels what I felt on June 4, 2014, in this judge's courtroom and be advised ineffectively and wrongfully during an election *lyfe"n"tyme*.

It's not Governor Beebe's fault. Our lawmakers need to be reformed and our police officers need to be reminded that being in a crispy blue uniform doesn't make it right to kill our black men. I put the paper down to get to my dental appointment in deep thoughts as I walked behind the yellow line.

My appointment was canceled until a later notice, which I was glad because today the menu consisted of chicken from what I heard. Due to my commissary restrictions the chow hall was much needed and of course the ladies made sure that I had whatever I wanted and needed. People outside of these walls, and even I have heard of all the prison sex stories for snacks. Yes it is happening, but you must be willing to do it.

Thinking back to ASU, we all love to give back to our community. Do we ever consider the colleges that I named before? What about the people in our community that have never attended college? Straight in front of me is an inmate name Stephanie, who is one of my favorite prisoners. She attended ASU and received a bachelor's degree in 2004, a master's degree in Special Education in 2006, and a second master's degree from ASU in 2011. Last night I watched her sleep so peacefully. What happens to these teachers who become sexually involved with their students? These young men's penis are probably only inches in measurement and feel no different than the small piece of chalk the teachers hold in their hands while solving problems on the blackboard. Ugh!

Stephanie is a citizen from Lonoke, Arkansas. She has spent all of her educational career between the Lonoke and Cabot school districts. What happens when the flesh is overtaken by the spirit of the carnal mind? Again, I tuned into the MP4 player listening to *"Put Your Hands on Me and Make my Body Go Boom Boom Boom!"* by Special.

I asked Stephanie who looked so innocent. "How did she become involved with a student?"

"Well, he was a friend of my son. He was seventeen and had been around my family for years. My husband worked a lot. We took a lot of trips with my son and him, they are both dirt bike riders, and it just happened." She explained.

"How did you two get caught?" I asked.

"Actually, his mother thought that I was having an affair with her husband because he owns an auto parts store in Cabot. He worked for his dad and I would be at the shop a lot. She later went through the phone records and found out it was her son and she was pissed off. This is my first time in prison or in any trouble. I have to do one more year. I might get denied my first time because of my charge, but his mother has written the parole board a letter and they're coming to support me. The mother feels that I've served my share of punishment." She answered.

I really enjoyed listening to Stephanie talk. She has such a sweet southern and country voice. I found myself looking up to this educated ASU college graduate. She told me her daughter is currently enrolled in ASU with a full scholarship. I shared the newspaper article about the love of Mike Beebe for ASU. I found myself talking a lot about our politics as I tuned into commercials and read newspaper articles. I watched Mike Ross, Tom Cotton, Mark Pryor, Asa Hutchinson, John Burkhalter, and even the commercials with Governor Beebe. I know each of us as prisoners may never be able to vote, but most of us have family members whose votes will matter. I plan to write, promote, and do whatever I possibly can to get from behind these white walls and campaign to the fullest during election time. It's not right what many court cases try to prove to our American voters during election time. I can honestly say this and I truly mean it GOD has his way in this *lyfe"n"tyme*!

I was told that the judge in my case made a comment a few days before his birthday in the early part of June 2014, that he would've given me more time if he could have. I guess it's possible even without no gun, no evidence, and no priors. It's been done. I still got sentenced to twenty-one years over a gap in my teeth.

Who am I? They must not know about me. My dad told them I am the Queen Bee. The name AngieSaidThat represents unity, trust me! I bring the city and different states out to my Arkansas events. The state of Arkansas doesn't know what type of talent they have sentenced to an unjust twenty-one years. I'm not a threat by far to people and my community knows it wholeheartedly. I'm not going to hurt a fly!

Justice, equality, and fairness will be granted to me in the natural state of Arkansas in Jesus name! AngieSaidThat

Chapter 6

Skittles

I looked up and watched another prisoner nicknamed Skittles, who is fighting brain cancer. She is a white female, short black hair, 5'4", 110 pounds, no top teeth and brown eyes. I noticed her talking and raising hell with Missy and Stephanie. Earlier, I watch them pack about $15 worth of items for the pill hustlers. It was three Nutty Buddy bars, about twenty envelopes, a pack of Skittles, beans, and a package of Kool-Aid. So what if the chocolate comes off the Nutty Buddy bar? Will Yo-Yo send another message about this transaction over a quarter ounce of missing chocolate? To witness this, take notes, but not report it to the warden, will this cost me another prisoner court appearance on commissary conspiracy charge?

AngieSaidThat reporting live in all white at Newport Prison from the bunk block of #32 and #33. An ASU master degree graduate, on bunk block #18, under indictment. If Skittles gets caught with the commissary money between her legs at pill call will this become a federal snack case?

This is my *lyfe"n"tyme* as a prisoner at Newport Prison. Ugh! I tuned into the song *"It Ain't the Whiskey"* by Gary Allan.

Chapter 7

Excuse me, Mr. Journalist!

I've watched prison movies and I've heard stories, but to be behind the prison walls in the midst of it all is still unreal to me. To watch one of my favorite actors, Denzel Washington, play the lead role in the true movie about Hurricane, the boxer, is truly an incentive to stay up writing. I would give anything to have recording cameras following my lyfe. Does our state know what type of money I would make and the ratings I would have just from my name itself?

It may be election time but I'm the winner! Even at the thought of the state fair, I am the roller coaster ride! I'm one of the best comedian, activist, mentor, spiritual guide, writer, sista/brotha, and simply one of the most multi-talented people in our state. Loved by plenty and wanted by many in all white facing twenty-one years in prison over a gap in my teeth with no priors and no gun, are you kidding me?

There are so many undercover issues going on and it is simply pitiful. Missy pulled her pants down below her waist to show me the carvings and cuttings in her skin where she carved Paige's name on her lower body part and on her fingers. Remind you this is another black stud in her life. She's now afraid that Paige is going to turn her into the staff after an argument over pills, so she went to the major to explain it herself. She assured the major that it was over with for sure.

The major expressed to her that she didn't care for biracial same-sex couples. She really doesn't approve of gay relationships, period. Many have told me about the racism against us as black homosexual studs. We are targeted! Well, many may complain, and three white studs even wanted to file a lawsuit for discrimination of homosexuality, unlike any blacks, who out of fear are afraid to do so. To try and get my very own people to stand with me is useless. Will this civil right movement place me in the pits of prison or in medical with lethal injections? I'm sure the prison will tell my family it was the flu shot that killed me or some other "natural cause".

I wonder if they are even reporting the truth about these deaths that have taken place within the last two years in this prison to our American people. I wonder why the water makes our mouths feel so dry. What type of chemicals are in the water with the same pipeline running concurrent in this prison?

We as prisoners perform all the work from the heating and air, plumbing, cleaning, laundry services, garden bed, field squad, kitchen and etc. I watched the operation of it all. I'm Inside Edition with the real story that inquiring minds want to know. "Extra, extra, read all about it! Live, with AngieSaidThat!"

I think about the journalist who really tried to get the public's attention with the article, *"Night Club Owner Found Guilty of '12 Bank Robbery"* after my jury trial. *"Sentenced to twenty-one years and must serve twelve before eligible for parole."*

Excuse me, Mr. Democrat Gazette writer! Excuse me! Were you out of ink? What about the gap and mustache? Did you also hear about the juror that dozed off? What about the juror that discussed the case in the hallway? What about not having a jury of my peers? And what about the hidden evidence, Mr. Journalist, around election time?

True enough, Mr. Journalist, you may have gone to school, Sir. And you may be very well educated to write without a doubt, but let's compare my forty-four cent commissary pen and my one dollar and fourteen cent legal writing pad to any story you have ever written for the State of Arkansas and compare it with not a newspaper article, but a series of books of truths and facts. Proven facts, not hearsay! I can say I am one of GOD's creations and I am blessed to do what most call the impossible. A text from my dear friend, Vona, revealed that it is my purpose in *lyfe "n" tyme*. Mr. Democrat Gazette, you are not the father, Boo-Boo!

I must remind most, I'm one of GOD's gifted creations. I know it's your job and you are going to get paid regardless. It's not your fault, and I will allow you to write about me again, but only real facts, Mr. Journalist. I know ways to get the public's attention too, and have them crave to read the best writer's material in town. Maybe people will start back buying the newspaper, Mr. Democrat Gazette newspaper writer, but then again, maybe not!

Trust me "I*t Ain't The Whiskey", a*s the song says and you can *"Blame it on Me."*

AngieSaidThat!

Chapter 8

Sugar Cookies

My series of books will sell like funnel cakes at the Arkansas State Fair! Just thinking back to the very first time I ever tasted one during my junior high school days brought a smile to my face. One of my favorite Home Economics teachers were Ms. Sharon Serio. She is a white female, 5'7", slim, big pretty brown eyes and the cutest dimples. She taught us to cook many different dishes. I can't say that I remember many of my teachers from Ridge Road Jr. High School, but to look over to bunk 18 and see Stephanie with a towel over her eyes surprises me. She is such a beautiful and educated woman, who never used drugs.

The fact of having sex with an active seventeen year old makes me feel some type of way and to be honest, some children are having sex at the age of twelve, babies at thirteen and fourteen, a grandmother by thirty. It may sound as if I'm lying, but most know I'm not. Now there are television shows about being sixteen and pregnant. There are plenty of white girls who are no longer sneaking off having abortions or secretly giving babies up for adoption. Parents are no longer sending their sons and daughters who are on drugs away until election time is over. Most know who I'm talking about. It is some of our elected officials, but it's not about them. It's about "Equality". People, stop thinking your children won't or shouldn't be in an all white uniform and the chaplain here in Newport flesh doesn't enjoy looking at these female fruit loops of all flavors. He's waiting for the moment of splash and squirt of the slippery when wet white milk to be added for the taste of it all, too. It truly does the body right. The flesh is taken over by the spirit of the carnal mind.

Unlike the former president from Arkansas, after he allowed Monica to give him a blow job and get a splash of milk on her dress.

He later apologized to the American people. We again voted him back in without a doubt. He never talked against what we truly needed in America. Sometimes we don't have to use tax payers dollars. He deserved that relief, no disrespect to them, but the truth has no defense. We all are only human at the end of the day and that's what needs to be understood the most. I talk about our chaplain, but he's only human. We as humans put many people on high pedestals, even me. I truly had a very uncontrollable gambling addiction and messed up, but GOD is a forgiving GOD. This shall pass in Jesus' name. Goodnight, pill call from Newport Prison. *"Shattered"* by Sevyn Streeter, lyrics are like throwing stones at a glass window.

Awaken always in prayers and praising Him. The fact of writing into the AM hours and unable to hear the breakfast calls over the noise of all the women lets me know how tired my body really is. I wanted to just hear from my sisters. The thought of a letter would be nice after nearly two weeks and Nana and Marilyn haven't responded back to my letters, but I noticed an officer that truly reminded me of my brother, Eric. My GOD all he need was to walk up to me asking for some money, cigarettes, and a six pack of beer! My brother, Eric is fifty years old, 5'5", 135 lbs., square head, flat face, and thin lips. Eyes of a drinker and truly a sweet man until the liquor kicked in. His behavior got very bad after our Mama died. It got even worse after our younger sister, DaShunda was killed and even worse after an older sister, Kim died of cancer. May they all Rest in Peace! They are all loved and truly missed.

I now wonder who Eric is calling besides me, Sharon, LaShay, and Nana, trying to get money for cigarettes and beer, or brag about his SNAP benefits, and the new love in his life every other week, not even knowing their last name. Most of his engagements consist of broken promises of marriage. Brotherly love through it all! I miss him begging now, but I won't later.

Officer Catfish walked around making rounds. He made me smile every time I saw him because he reminded me so much of my brother, even though he is white. He stopped by our bed and reached into Missy's bunk taking three peppermints and sliding them in his pocket. I took one behind him.

He looked at me and said. "Richardson, you know that's a major write up getting into another prisoner's trunk." He stated.

"You know it's your job to be in a prisoner's trunk eating their commissary, Sir." I replied smiling.

They all laughed at me reciting the rules so shortly after my prison court appearance in Newport Prison. Mr. Catfish is truly one of the good guys around here. Which really help us as prisoners get through situations like mine, facing twenty-one unjustified years.

I wasn't going to be able to afford a private attorney and even I, myself, was lost on the legal representation of it all. Why did I even think my appointment of counsel would help me? I know GOD will send me somebody. This is no longer my battle, it is the Lord's! I have to focus on my purpose in *lyfe "n" tyme even* while facing twenty-one unjustified years.

Sgt. Era walked in yelling hit your racks! He had in his hand a tool with a long tube and a small light attached to the end of it and behind him stood a female officer with gloves. Again, he screamed. "Hit your racks now!"

He searched the sink, showers, and pulled up the shower curtains. He searched and searched. What led to this search?

Two black inmates exchanged words in the chow hall earlier. A black stud name Sta-Day, 5'7", 280 lbs., light skinned, low haircut faded on the side with tattoos, and a gap in her teeth and Meaka, 5'6", glasses, dark skinned, 280 lbs., black hair below her neck, and she loved to talk. She runs her mouth like Pac-Man with an energizer battery. Ugh!

I sat in the chow hall listening to the argument. Meaka had asked several times for more sugar cookies and meatballs. I knew Meaka from our former hair stylist, who is one of Little Rock's best stylist. She's something else here in prison!

Meaka touched upon a very sensitive subject as they started arguing after Skittles, the inmate with brain cancer, handed Sta-Day a sugar cookie and said. "Here, Bro."

"She is not a boy." Meaka replied. "She is a woman just like us and these studs get anything and everything around here." She was really mad over something she didn't need. EXTRA COOKIES... UGH!

"Look, don't worry about what I am. I look damn good with yo fat ass." Stay-Day replied.

"Fat? Look, girl you are fat and on top of that, yo body built bad and I mean BAD!" Meaka argued and as she watched Sta-Day eat the cookies she got even more heated.

"That's because I lift weights and the only thing you are lifting is a meatball off yo tray." Sta-Day argued steaming mad over Meaka's comments about her body. They began to get extremely loud. Returning back to Barrack 13, the argument continued. I finally pulled Sta-Day to the side once they got close enough to fight.

"Look, Lil Bro, we will be judged for the rest of our lives about our lifestyle and especially being a black gay stud. So, allow people to talk. It's not worth getting into more trouble than what we already are in by being here." I explained. "Bro, we are already in prison and these people hate us damn near over our homosexuality. Please just chill Lil' Bro." I asked smiling.

"You're right, Angie, thank you!" She replied smiling and walked off placing her radio plugs in her ears to avoid arguing.

Skittles yelled. "Yes, I called the police in here and told them that Meaka might have hidden cigarettes and I don't give a damn who's mad. I'm dying anyway and I will take a bitch out with me. I'm on my last leg and I ain't sorry!"

Once the officer left the Barrack, the chaos turned up. The prisoners really hated snitches. Skittles apparently didn't appreciate all the gay comments and wanted to cause trouble for Meaka by snitching that she may have cigarettes.

I really didn't understand her reasons for telling the police, but Meaka admitted to me last night that she had cigarettes and asked me if I smoked. I thank GOD that I never had the desire to smoke. The noise and arguments went on for a while. I calmed a few people down, but Meaka went on and on like the energizer bunny. She wouldn't stop over a sugar cookie! Are you kidding me? The sugar cookies have energized her flesh. Ugh!

I looked over at Skittles as she laid on her bunk listening to her radio obviously tuning out the noise. Missy was listening to T.I. on her MP4 player as she looked in the mirror rubbing conditioner in her hair.

I looked over to my left as inmates Kecia Pannell and Moe Sharp laid on their bunks and shook their heads. Kecia is a character within herself.

Kecia is light skinned, short hair, 5'6'', 125 lbs., a gap in her teeth, and reminded me so much of Blacklace, a well-known transgender whom our community very much missed. Dennis Randolph "AKA" Blacklace, may you rest in peace.

Kecia has been back and forth to Newport Prison. She told me when we talked a few days earlier that her aunt and uncle raised her and she had the best of the best during her teenage years until her mother interfered in the midst of her life.

She enjoyed and loved the game of basketball. All she ever wanted to do was play basketball. It was something that her aunt and uncle allowed her to do daily and she claimed them as her parents.

In 2009, she served eleven months for residential burglary. She admits that once her mother removed her out of a good environment she started to get involved with drugs and trouble. Her mother made her quit school in the 12th grade and she stopped playing basketball. Until this day she has not yet received her GED. After she was taken away from her aunt she no longer cared about life. Her dreams of being a basketball player never came to be. She started hanging out with other troubled teens and with the wrong surrounding of people. She got to the point where she had no problem asking her mama for drugs to get high and smoked crack at an early age. She became very unstable in her life moving from place to place all the time, sometimes they didn't have a place to go. Kecia, became bitter on the inside and later at the age of 16, she finally got the chance to meet her father someone that was a stranger in her *lyfe"n"tyme*. Her father started sending her clothes from Las Vegas. Fashions that she wasn't use to in her *lyfe"n"tyme* during the years that she spent with her aunt and uncle.

I asked Kecia, what is it now that she wanted to change in her *lyfe* versus coming back and forth to prison spending her *lyfe"n"tyme*. She told me that she wanted to become a nurse and that she really wanted to save her younger brothers and sisters from experiencing the same *lyfe* that she had. Kecia also admitted she wants to still do drugs, not crack, but other drugs such as blunts and pills. I'm not one to judge, but she loved the way drugs make her feel. I pray for her strength and I also advised her to continue participating in school programs once she is on the outside of these white walls. I advised her to get back focused and when she receives her GED, to get into a college program. I'm asking my readers to keep everyone here in Newport Prison in your prayers. Kecia has great potential, but I still see and understand the bitterness, anger, and hurt within her. GOD hears our cries behind the bars of these white walls. In Jesus name.

Chapter 9

Meaka

Thirty minutes later, I looked up at inmate Meaka as she walked over to hand me a letter wanting to share the deep feelings within her mind and spirit. We all have a story to tell, although most have no intentions of writing about theirs. However, I'm blessed to be able to share to the stories of others like Meaka.

"My anger and resentment all started with my mother. My mother had ten children. Four were born with alcohol fetal syndrome, two were stillborn, and she had one miscarriage. Seven of us were supposed to be born normal, but I still feel as if we were all affected in some way.

I grew up hating my mother because I couldn't understand what she was going through and how a mother could not love her children. Until I got older. My mother destroyed our lives. I always felt like she never cared and didn't give a damn who she gave us to. She gave four of my siblings away to my great aunt, Marle Gamble, who was almost a senior citizen herself at the time. She couldn't care for four children, but she did the best she could.

My siblings became extremely wild at a young age, having company over at all times of the night and having sex, and running the streets. She couldn't handle the children. Two of them were mentally retarded. No matter what, they were my sisters and brothers and I always wanted to be with them. I constantly ran away to be with them. My mother gave me away to her brother, William. I hated living with him because he married Lee Hunt and her children mistreated me so badly. He did to at times. I was overwhelmed with feeling unloved, unwanted, and mentally and physically abused. I thought that if I could only be with my siblings everything would be better. Boy, was I ever wrong! Running away to be with them didn't help the situation at all. It only exposed me more to the street life. Not that I wasn't already going through enough where I was living.

My mom was a drunk and she was born mentally retarded. I didn't understand her condition until I was grown. My uncle didn't protect me either. Uncle William ended up with three of us, two of my brothers and me.   Cornelius and Drew were both severely mentally retarded. They got it the worse because they couldn't talk and they have the minds of three and four year olds, if not younger. Really seeing them took a lot out of me. Watching and caring for my sibling made me more depressed. I was deeply wounded with so many issues myself and there was nothing I could do for them. I was in need of help! I needed someone to come rescue me at a very young age. I was physically abused by my mother and my aunt. I was also molested by several different family members on her side of the family. When I told nothing was done about it. A lot of the molestation in my family went untold.

Like for instance when my aunt's brother, Willie, had me in his bedroom humping, grinding, and rolling around on top of me in his bed with my clothes on. No one would come looking for me, or wondered where I was. I never told it. Then there was a time when her nasty perverted nephew, Steve, use to take me to the peach field in the back of my aunt's sister, Nita, house.   Several times a day he took me back there as if we were picking fruit and I hated it, but I never said anything. These occurrences happen when I was at the ages four, five and maybe six. All I know is that I was extremely young. Then there was this old man who use to pretend he was fixing the zipper on my pants, but he was actually playing with my vagina. I never said anything, but get this! He wasn't related to me and I found myself wondering all the time over to his house. His name was Mr. Bob. He was nice and he never abused me in any other kind of way. I liked him because he was nice and would also feed me when I went over there. It was somewhere I could get away to and have some peace, but when I would return home all hell would break loose. Nothing but chaos!

I often found myself wishing that GOD would take me away. I started hating and cursing GOD because I felt he wasn't protecting me. I found myself very contradicting when it came to GOD. I was truly battling through heaven and hell. At a young age the devil took hold of me, but GOD refused to let go. I now know GOD never took his arms from around me when I was going through hell growing up. My mother was nowhere to be found. She only came around every blue moon and that was only because she needed some rest in order to recuperate and then go back to the streets with Lord knows who. To my knowledge, my mother never smoked cigarettes or used drugs. She only had a problem with alcohol and men and I'm not saying that isn't a bad thing. By twenty-eight years old, I told myself that I would be different by not drinking.

Instead I started smoking crack but I didn't get high with my children.

My life has been very painful till this day. I found myself crying a river because of my life. My mother didn't show me affection when she left and I didn't feel anything. I remember her pouring black pepper in my eyes which my Aunt Ora found funny. Sometimes my aunt would provoke my mom to do bad things to me. My mom use to tell me that she hated me. My aunt and her children would often express their hatred for me. Until this day, I'm not liked very much by people, so to me there is something going on inside of me that has been going on for a long time, something that makes people not like me. All my life I felt rejected. I have never felt loved and felt sorry for myself. Today, I am 36 years old, soon to be 37 in a couple of days. My life hasn't consisted of anything but making poor decisions. I've been in and out of institutions, foster care and jails. You name it and I have been through it.

Today, I'm trying to change, but people don't have any faith in me because I have such a track record of making foolish decisions. I don't care what others think, I have enough faith in myself. People are not going to see the good in me anyway.

But, back to my mother, it seems as if I lost myself for a minute. Anyhow, like I said in the beginning of this letter my mother was a drunk and mentally retarded. In my twenties, my anger and resentment started fading a way towards my mother. I was starting to see things a bit more clearly thanks to GOD. He presented to me a clear image of my mother's mother. I never thought about my grandmother being an alcoholic. GOD reminded me of how my grandmother's living room had tall cans of Miller's beer scattered everywhere. I then began to understand where my mom's addiction came from. My mom was only doing what she had seen all her life. My grandmother owned a duplex and she lived on one side and allowed my mother to live on the other side. There's no telling what went on at my mother's side of the house. All I know is that she had several children and didn't know who any of our fathers were. No man came forth to claim any of her children. I stopped being so mad at my mom because she herself had it bad. My mom was misused and abused by men leaving her pregnant and not helping her. Someone once almost killed my mom. It truly broke my heart seeing her like that. I wondered what kind of animal would do her like that and I never understood what kind of man would be interested in a mentally retarded woman anyway, plus she was an alcoholic. What a dirty dog!

My other two sisters were ashamed of our mother. One of my sisters despised her so much she will not claim her til this day. I tried explaining to her about mama, but she didn't want to hear it.

When I started reading the alcohol anonymous book and going to meetings and learning the serenity prayer, I really let down all my guards towards my mother. I fully let go of resentments, but I held on to the resentment for others. I got into my fourth step. I remember my uncle's wife son, Curtis, had a small video game. It was a trip to play Pac-Man. We each had to line up outside with the door closed waiting on our time while the other one finished playing. Well, when it was my turn, I found out I wasn't in there to play the game. I was only in there for him to molest and fondle all over my body. I never told anyone. I was mad at mom for not being there and allowing all this to happen to me. I was being physically and mentally abused. Today, I forgive my mom, but we still don't have a relationship.

In 2012, when I got out of prison I saw her at the Little Rock bus station. I spoke and it kind of hurt my feelings that she never spoke back to me. I also later remembered the time after I had my son and was showing my baby to my mother. She spit in my face. My mother had a very bad habit of spitting in people faces.

I never received any happy birthday or holiday gifts from my mother. She was inactive in my life and it hurt me growing up. I didn't have anybody in my life and it has been nothing but pain and misery. In my fourth step telling about my uncle and mom and their crazy households, there is no telling how many pages I needed to write. There's so much that happened in my life and I actually find writing quite healing. I should have done this a long time ago. I didn't know I could release a lot of what's been hindering me on paper and writing helps me to sort things out. I will forever be writing. I don't know if it will help every situation, but it's definitely a beginning for me. Thank you, Angie, for sharing my story in your book!

Chapter 10

Meaka's Uncle

I stopped writing to read Meaka's story. In the midst of writing this story my heart was saddened and I suddenly needed to cry on the inside, but I didn't allow the tears to run down my face even though they formed in my eyes. I tuned in listening to Whitney Houston's version of *"His Eyes Is on the Sparrow"*.

I had no control of GOD's purpose for me at this point in my *lyfe "n" tyme*. I hit repeat and tuned everything out behind these white walls from the arguments, chow-time, rec time, other prisoners, commissary, and staff, to being unable to call my wife. Meaka was from a family of ten and so was I, but our mama was most surely our hero. To have lost her on May 10, 2000, to cancer turned my world upside down. To have another prisoner ask me to share her story with my readers, leads me to *Tri GOD: Now & Later"*. Angiesaidthat!

I took a break just long enough to fix me another cup of tea and get my assigned bunk #33 comfortable enough to write with purpose in Jesus name. I thought of my dear friend, Vona Cox, text message asking me. "What is your purpose in "lyfe"? I wished that I had a cell phone at this moment. I would send her a one word reply. *GOD!*

Shortly after taking a break from writing, I took two of my vitamins and a Tylenol to help ease the pain in my lower back from sitting on the iron bunk and thin mat. And to know that Jesus experienced much worse trying to protect us! Secretly, I kept me a few Tylenol 3's inside my Lay's potato chip bag which gave my pain pills a little flavor. So, maybe I need to write Lay's about all these "Lay's potato chips pills". Cough harder... LOL! UGH!

I continued writing Meaka's story about her *lyfe "n" tyme.*

Well, at this part of my fourth step, I'm going to share with you something regarding me and my uncle. My uncle was married to Lee Hunt. She had six children when she met him, six snotty nose children, as my Uncle Freddy would say. They had a total of nine. She also had one by my uncle's best friend, Harry.

Either my uncle knew about his friend screwing his wife and downright accepted it or said the hell with it. He accepted the child and was too ashamed to tell anybody. He never confronted his wife or his best friend. There were never any disputes or questions from him regarding the child outside of their marriage. Even Stevie Wonder could've seen this child wasn't my uncles, but anyway I knew about the child being Harry's. I harbored this secret for the longest not sharing it with anyone, until later in my teenage years. I wanted to tell my uncle who Lee's baby daddy really was, but instead I decided to tell Harry's wife over the phone. I asked her why she didn't tell my uncle. However, he died not really knowing.

I listened to one of my favorite artist, Sir Charles, songs titled *"Just Can't Let Go"*, while writing this part of Meaka's story. The lyrics very well had me in my own zone. *"I just can't let go. I never missed one day of work. I never denied her the least little thing. I'm a father to the children, sometimes I cook the food, bring home all my money. Let her do want she wanna do, but I can't let go. Everybody down the line some here been a fool."* Meaka's story continued.

My uncle died at the age of 36 years old. I remember sitting on the porch with my uncle, which we hardly ever did. We never had any quality time together. I remember sitting on the back porch telling him how I felt about the way she mistreated him, me, and my brothers. The thoughts of his wicked wife and as a man he had no backbone. I told him I wasn't going to stay, but he could if he wanted to. So, he didn't have to come look for me anymore, I told him if he didn't leave he was going to die and the age of 36 he did. I was around 11 or 12 when I predicted this. Anyhow, I was 16 when my uncle died.

I was so hurt because I know my uncle died with a broken heart. After he died, I started having children at a young age. I was finally in my own abusive relationship and I kinda understood where he was coming from. Once again GOD had made it where things had become a lot clearer to me. Even till this day I often think about my uncle and I miss him. I know he loved me. Today, I do know that. I didn't know growing up. His wife didn't allow him to love us. He even threw my mentally disabled brother in the pool trying to make a man out of him knowing he wasn't able to swim. The way he treated us allowed me to see a weakened man. My uncle stayed high. The days he wasn't drinking he was with her and their children scamming. She was a con artist. He worked indeed whatever to support his wife and children. He really took his marriage seriously.

I can't begin to describe in detail to my readers how my stomach felt to read and write this story. As I listened to Sir Charles song, *"Better or Worse"* and the lyrics *"we traded vows and now my heart is hurt, you suppose to love me"*, I continued to write Meaka's story.

My uncle told me they adopted me at the age of nine months. Between foster care and the streets, it's a wonder I'm not dead. I may as well be. I ain't accomplished nothing. My life hasn't been nothing but jails, prisons and drama. The only thing left is death. Lord, I hope not. I remember as a little girl, my uncle would get me ready for school. I remember he used to wash my face from the spit out his mouth. I would turn my head back and forth trying to prevent him from doing it. I would be like yuck!

He would tell me to shut up, but I know he wanted to hit me. I wanted to stay with my real family. My aunt also would get me to fight my sister, Jean, whenever I would go to see them. My Aunt Ora was a drama queen and love to keep up mess. So, she always got us to fight so they would hate me. She didn't want nobody to love me. My uncle and his wife would load me and all the other kids up in the same vehicle. We were packed like sardines and everybody would be on top of one another. Some of us would even have to sit up front on my aunt's lap. We would be very uncomfortable, but anyway we would be fully loaded and going off to hustle. They would take us to the white folk's neighborhood, as they would call it. They would have already laid down the guideline as to what we were supposed to do and mainly it would be him going to the doors with all of us to get some money.

We would go from door to door and come up with the most outrageous lies as to why we were in need of money. We would say somebody in the family died and we didn't have any money or insurance to pay for a funeral, or our house burned down. At a young age I learned how to scam, con, get over, and turn into a criminal.

To me he needed to put on a dress and her in a pants suit. She even kicked his ass and when her kids got older they helped her. I prayed many times he would hit her back. One time she slapped him with a hot sauce bottle and busted his head open. He chased her but couldn't catch her.

At times I took her side because I was scared and trembling in my boots. I even joined in helping her fight my uncle. Inside I was praying and wanting him to fight us back. I was so sad inside. Because I felt so bad for him, I never told my uncle I didn't mean any of it. I was only between the ages of seven through nine. My uncle would chase me and what he wanted to do to his wife he'd do it to me. He would hurt me, bust my mouth, slap me and whatever it was he wanted to do to her, but too afraid to.

I remember her cutting a bald spot in his hair and painting his face with her makeup and throwing cake flour in his face. She wanted to get a reaction out of him. He cried wanting to know why she did him like that and I wondered why in the hell she hurt her husband like that. He had to wear a hat for a while. May GOD rest his soul! I don't know, but maybe God knows by allowing him to die and leave her. She later would appreciate him. She was horrible. It's like she found herself lost in love by his spirit, but his flesh was long gone back to dust.

As I continued to write Meaka's story, I tuned in to the song, *"One Wing"* by Jordan Sparks.

Chapter 11

Stephanie

"Chow-time!" the officer yelled on September 24, 2014, at 6:10 PM, as we waited for the door to open for six black prisoners. A.D., a black dark chocolate cute stud, Kecia, a dancing machine, Sta- Day, Lynn, Boosie, and Moni, the talented one who is able to make magical beats with a small ink pen. I stood on the side nodding my head thinking about Charlie Wilson and Quincy Jones and how a great producer or an artist is able to see the spiritual talents of people. I enjoyed the thoughts and visions of when my books are released and the day that I will be able to invite certain prisoners in front of people to witness what they most fear, prisoners! And what most prisoners fear from society, judgment! We need a chance to show and share our purposes in our *lyfe"n"tyme.*

By all means, I wholeheartedly agree there are certain people in here at Newport Prison that I would not care to have or want around me, my nieces, or other family members, just the same as some of you who walk outside these prison walls. Most are some of your very own family, coworkers, classmates, lawmakers, neighbors, and church members. I must admit I've also met some very caring, loyal, and good people in Newport Prison. I've met so many people with great talents.

I picked up the paper and read about the election. I've seen commercials with Mike Ross walking down college hallways. Do people know that we need lawmakers that don't just focus on education? We are already aware that our youth need to be college educated. This has been taught and talked about from politicians and our parents for years!

We need our American people to know that our community, from the rags of the hood, to the soft fabric of the middle class, to the softest cow skin of the rich, is not always about the American dollar. Most of these horses that are out of the barn are calling out the jockeys to ride in on a vote.

It's time for our state to change its old fashion ways of thinking and as Christians love others as GOD loves us.

To pick up the paper and read about our governor's great heart to donate to ASU is interesting. I've talked with an inmate with a bachelor's degree and two master degrees from ASU and her father is employed at BMW of Little Rock. He loves his daughter just as much as everyone loves their child. Sometimes money can't save a person from serving time, but as a politician you are able to make phone calls to make things happen. But with GOD all things are possible and she deserves a pardon.

Stephanie, an ASU graduate, dropped out of her program here at Newport which may cause her to be denied in front of the parole board. It's called "SOFT", the Sex Offender Female Treatment program. The experts told her that she's manipulative and has a way of getting what she wants from her father and others. She looks at it differently. Her father does his best at the BMW dealership and will do whatever it takes to sell the best made foreign cars. She looks up to her dad. The fact is she's more educated then the experts, but her experiences do not make her anything but who she is in reality. This woman is human and she allowed her flesh to desire a young seventeen year old young man, who was already sexually active. We cannot see into the future, but does this make her a monster and a sex offender for the rest of her *lyfe "n" tyme*?

I looked over at her and she said smiling. "Angie, I have something for you. I remember yesterday how you talked about how much you love her and was attracted to her even in *"The Color Purple"* movie as Sophia. So, I want you to have this month's issue. My family sends them to me sometimes." She said smiling as she handed me the "O" magazine.

The gap in my teeth was again revealed, but not to a jury trial. Due to fact of me really loving Oprah, I couldn't write anymore. I flipped through the pages of the "O" magazine. I looked at one of ASU smartest students, Stephanie, and said.

"This magazine means just as much as what our governor donated. Thank you so much! You don't know how this makes me feel, Stephanie. The fact that you even thought about me and how I feel about Oprah, this is like a birthday gift!" I said smiling and we both laughed.

"O" Magazine.

See life through new lens! How to love all your quirks! Love your flaws! Celebrate your style! Relax! Reset! Revive! O's guide to beating burnout.

To open up the first page and see one of the most beautiful black women in the city of Chicago. "The taste of Chicago". Quotes at the bottom read; "Every woman needs a little mystery and a lot of color."

I tuned into the MP4 player listening to *"Beautiful"* by Eminem. I was feeling every lyric in this song as I excitedly flipped to the next page looking at Oprah. She is covered in red fabric, lavender stone diamonds, one nice ring placed on her ring finger and another one placed on her middle finger, dark color nail polish and a nice pair of earrings. Everything just blended together. Her makeup was done to perfection on her face. Her skin was just as smooth as a newborn baby's booty. Well, it's no other term I could use to explain to my readers. A baby's booty is so soft and beautiful. Even in prison she made me feel some type of way.

I finally flipped the page. Her teeth were just as white as the paint behind these prison walls. She was dressed in all white.

Unbelievable! The smile topped any toothpastes, white strips, or dentist commercials that I've ever seen in my life. At the bottom it read; *"When in doubt, be bold!" "O"*

As, I flipped the pages, I focused only on her photos and quotes. I tuned into *"Never Love Again"* by Anthony Hamilton, and looking down at the photos and reading the quotes, *"What's life without some sparkle?"* Oprah placed both hands on each side of her face. Her eyes are so beautiful with diamond stones across her eyebrows and her fingers. The smile gave her face small cute creases on each side. The breeze of the windy city. *"O"*

Again, turning the pages, I dreamed of writing for *"O"* one day. John Legend's *"All of Me"* took me there without any disrespect to her mate and by all means after all, I am a lesbian. Oprah had me appreciating the reasons of not regretting my lifestyle. I never pushed my lifestyle on anyone, but I do have what this next page speak of with four beautiful photos of her, dramatic eyes and bold lips.

True enough I don't have any Kohl eyeliner or extravagant lashes, but as I quickly flipped through the other pages to search for another page of *"O"* it finally reads; *"Here We Go"*! At the bottom with an article to the left of it, but I'm unable to read it on this bunk with very little light. I could very well see the quotes though;" *As it turns out, none of us is "normal"…which means that all of us are."*

I turned the page again and couldn't keep my eyes off of my *"O" Magazine* and my mind was so many miles away from this place. I wasn't sure what type of bird this was, but the pointed tip of the mouth was to the right, it had somewhat of a yellow and dark brown coat with mint green colored feet. One foot was placed on a stone, the other foot was held as if it was in a birdie Olympics position. The quote above read;" *Live your best life."* The bottom read; *"But you...you are you, and now isn't that pleasant? Dr. Seuss!"*

As I continued to look at the photos, I wasn't able to listen to the one song on the MP4 player that I needed to take me there as I stared at the photo. *"I Believe I Can Fly"* by R. Kelly. I do know GOD can do the impossible as I closed the *"O" Magazine.*

I took a moment to drop down on my knees to pray about meeting her and that my books one day become a part of her book club, and to have a chance to write for *"O" Magazine* in Jesus name.

I had to be careful of my prayers and submit in a respectful way to our Creator. Oprah said at Maya Angelo's home going celebration that *"behind every cloud is a rainbow."* One of Maya Angelo's New York Times best sellers, *"Wouldn't Take Nothing for My Journey Now"* is right here in the Newport Prison Library. I have it and it motivates me to write all night. However, she did quote years ago, *"I Rise and Still I Rise."* I will never forget one of my longtime friends, Cassandra Walker, running for Miss Philander Smith College and doing that speech for her talent. I rise even in the midst of the officers yelling at hundreds of prisoners and staff. What GOD has for you in your *lyfe"n"tyme* nobody can take it in Jesus name! I will be careful of how I pray *now & later* with *the cries behind the bars.*

Chapter 12

We Gettin' a Good Christmas Bonus!

The prayer that caused tears that I couldn't control as the red light flashed for the 12:30 AM count time. We all know GOD is a busy man and even Jesus has his hands full with us, every second and every minute with our issues on a daily basis. This prayer made me feel some type of way. I tuned in to one of the songs that have become one of my favorites with my upper bunk mate, Missy's MP4 player. *"It Ain't the Whiskey"* by Gary Allan.

I wrapped up, trying to remain warm in such a cold place. I looked over at the last toilet in Barrack 13 and saw a blanket over the top of it. It was full of waste and one of the prisoners had placed a blanket over the top of it a few weeks ago. To have been moved into this Barrack where there were some things I just didn't understand regarding the problems in our living conditions and not to mention the comments I overheard on July 16, 2014, my first day here.

A few staff member in the intake area was laughing and talking saying. "We're overcrowded and surely we will be getting a good Christmas bonus. We don't have to worry about that this year." They all giggled to see the prison overcrowded!

One thing I do know is that GOD makes no mistakes. Once he creates any of us, we have a purpose in our *lyfe "n" tyme*. It's no mistake in Jesus name that He allowed my books to be mailed out of this prison with facts from a creative writer and her commissary ink pen. True enough prisoners and officers all have witnessed me up until the AM hours writing. I will have time to get plenty of sleep later, but until then I will make sure that AngieSaidThat name will never be forgotten. I didn't write my books just about me. I freely acknowledge GOD's children too. True, people will have their say so and most lawmakers will try and belittle my work, but I'm not trying to get any votes. I'm simply trying to help our people realize that all that glitters ain't gold. Now, that I'm free of my gambling addiction, I'm on the right team *now & later.*

GOD has taken me back and signed me over to his championship team. The same as the razorback player, Collins, took the ball with the Arkansas Razorbacks touchdown, the same as Derrick Fisher, who is now a super good coach, the same as Joe Johnson, who make unbelievable basketball plays, the same as my cousin, Joe Adams, will continue to touch and bless a football, the same as Nikki Parish's voice touched many at the Apollo, the same as Playa Mook, a comedian, bring laughter to others in the state of Arkansas. There are many greatly blessed and talented people such as myself.

The courtroom didn't think so, but GOD's verdict is different. He overrules it all. This is his earth and all his creations. We are on borrowed *tyme "n" lyfe.* My books don't lie. I urge you to *Tri GOD: Now & Later.*

I don't know one person in American history that has been sentenced to twenty-one unjustified years over a gap in their teeth, with no evidence, no priors and a history of great deeds in our community to have written four books in less than four months. Plus, currently studying the law to be able to write their very own appeal and also help other prisoners with their legal paperwork.

True enough, Stanley is one of Arkansas's best attorneys but being indigent I had no choice but to study numerous law books for myself.   I tip my hat off to all attorneys and their fees. I understand why my appointed counsel made the statement, "I'm going to get paid regardless" and I now realized she worked with the prosecutors on my case.

So many people are afraid to take anything outside of a plea deal with an appointed counsel, but what about the people who are unable to read and have no understanding of the law? And what about those who are unable to buy a commissary dictionary to break the meaning down like a perm on a nappy head, and have nobody to help them? Most people aren't blessed with a personality and sense of humor such as mine and have a frog's mentality. I have witnessed so many frogs outside in the garden leaping around quietly trying to find their directions. The frogs faithfully rely on GOD!

I will keep pushing and praying until Something Happens! It's all about my conviction of the gap and the cries behind the bars in New Port prison. It's now called Lyfe "n" Tyme "and Tri GOD: Now & Later. AngieSaidThat!

Chapter 13

Throwing Stones at a Glass House

I thought about how my class got busted and getting moved to what most inmates refer to as a wild Barrack for accepting stationary material from AB. I thought about it and decided it wasn't her fault, even though she has been behind these walls for eighteen years. She most definitely knows the rules. The fact of her being nice and attracted to me caused her to break the rules, regardless. The thought of Warden Frances calling me ignorant due to the fact I was unaware of the policy on trafficking and trading, saying her youngest daughter knows better, and she would like to think I'm smarter than that had me feeling some type of way. The conversation and statements played in my head over and over. I get so sick of people asking me if I have been to the hole and telling me if I got three major write-ups it would affect my appeal, and that AB is talking bad about me now. The news and rumors traveled faster than a western union wire transfer behind these bars.   We all know bad news travels much faster than anything positive.

I chose not to reply back to certain negative people. I wasn't sure what AB said to others and to be honest I very well stopped King Avenue from telling me about the he say/she say. I am far from Warden Frances youngest daughter and to have the major cut me short and not even listen to anything I had to say was insulting, especially with what I see as some of their standards.

I clearly understand why so many inmates are back here after only six months of parole with the professional experts, who are over the programs, methods of helping to reform certain inmates, such as Stephanie. The Chaplain program and the drug program are a waste of time and taxpayers money. These programs are not rehabilitating the inmates. There are much better ways our lawmakers can make a difference. And another question, if commissary and inmate council sales are so beneficial, then why can't we have ice or bottled water behind these bars?

I'm simply stating the facts, but who am I to listen to? I'm just an ignorant black gay female with the mindset of a young child here in Newport Prison walking behind the yellow line, hands down, no talking, with nappy hair, because according to Officer Ox, "Black folks don't have hair like that." Ugh!

Missy made a statement earlier after she came back from classification. She stated, "I have a pending D.R. for talking in the hall, but I'm going to tell the major I'm done talking to black studs. The major told me the only reason I will get my D.R. dropped depends on who I was talking to in the hallway."

Of course this is much unlike my very first mistake, which got my class busted and 20 days of restrictions. A.B. also received the same restrictions, but she was class one, which meant she remained in the same Barrack, just unable to shop commissary, have visits, or use the telephone. I have zero understanding of her reason for being mad at me. She needs to listen to *"Shattered"* by Sevyn Streeter, with the lyrics, *"you keep pointing fingers, it's like we throwing stones at a glass house."* Angiesaidthat!

To hear other prisoners say how they got a warning on their first D.R., no matter if it was a major or a minor, was puzzling to me. Even the ASU graduate's D.R. disappeared after her dad made a few phone calls. My mama always told me sometimes it's not what you know, but who you know in your *lyfe "n" tyme*.

The real truth of the matter is the staff pretty much allow those who have been here long term to get by with certain behaviors, but the rules of the handbook applies to an inmate such as myself.

Chapter 14

(SMH) Shaking My Head...Ugh!

One thing that I am use to in this prison, from hosting many diversity events and being an activist in our community, is all the talking, gossiping, rumors, and peoples thoughts about me. I'm very well use to those who are concerned about whether I am in the hole or not and of those who really wished I was in the hole. Many studs claim to be everything, but themselves. They deny the fact of giving birth to children. They fall out with each other over females and they talk bad about each other.

Hershey claimed that she pulled a gun on me and had problems with me, and all of it boils down to one thing, lies. It reminds me of envious people wanting to walk in AngieSaidThat shoes, even in prison. SMH...Shaking My Head!

Where I am today is no accident. GOD is using me in this situation. We are all in here right now to shape and prepare us for the next place in our *lyfe"n"tyme*. Let's trust him *now & later,* because His plans work even if we don't understand them.

Like I have told numerous people, please feel free to ask me about AngieSaidThat because nobody, but GOD, can tell you better than me. Just because you have been to my club or my events don't mean you know me. You know of me and there is a big difference! It's called *lyfe"n" tyme*.

3:30 AM

I'm unable to sleep and I just finished writing my wife. I needed her to believe in my book series. I constantly try to tell her about my spirit, hopes and prayers. Her job keeps her so stressed out, and sometimes I wonder if the shoe was on the other foot, would I be pecking on the computer every chance I got to make her movement happen. I'm currently on phone restriction and unable to call her. It's very irritating!

My wife may not feel how I feel about my journey, because after all it is my purpose, but she enjoys reading my books. I constantly explain that I'm not up writing all night to have my material just sitting around although others have claimed they will help type them. The facts of my gifted creations in books will bring so much attention to our state and lawmakers. I need justice fairly served. If she does not get these books typed it can't possibly be a future for us. She might as well marry her job, no matter how much I love her. She claims that she's my backbone. These books are the bone in my back and spirit. My wife admits how she's so attracted to Ellen. Well, there is no telling who we might get a chance to meet and everybody who claims to know me, know that I love Prince and Oprah. As the gays say… yeeesss, hunni!

Today, three other prisoners asked me to share their stories. So many want to be a part of my book and share their stories of their lyfe "n"tyme. Stanley did advise people that I'm the Queen Bee in our community, but due to the fact that I'm black and gay, unlike a former Little Rock coach who got probation for killing his friend, I damn near got the lethal injection.

Not to mention in the year of 2006, I was taken to jail every Saturday night over beer and Quality House Vodka by Little Rock narcotic agents, on the strength of me providing a safe place for us to be as the black gay community.

Again, *"Blame it on me. Say it's my fault. I really don't care. I ain't crying no more.* GOD needed to use me more than any of you. He's not bias or prejudice, and he's the jury of my homosexual peers. My life made no sense as I was searching all doors for my release, but my faith, hope and prayers are granted in Jesus name. Thinking of my unanswered questions as I listen to Trey Songz' *"Gotta Go",* I know these prisoners think I'm out my mind and probably need to be in the Pill Call line getting meds. But, GOD is the cure to my sleeplessness, *now & later.* Trust me, this is freedom for me until GOD opens these doors and release me. My faith, hope, and prayers are granted in Jesus name. AngieSaidThat

I couldn't stop writing or thinking about others especially, my wife. I started listening to *"I Gotta Be"* by Jagged Edge, thinking about her and feeling all the lyrics. *"I gotta be the one you feel, I gotta be the one to fill your life with sunshine, don't ever want you to go nowhere, you make me whole, you make me right now."* Ugh, if she don't get my books typed, she will be listening to *"I'd Rather Be Blind"* by Etta James. AngieSaidThat!

I looked up and noticed A.D. tuned into a MP4 player and singing. She reminded me so much of the young man who played in *"Love & Basketball."* She's chocolate, big eyes, dimples and cute. She is 25 years old and a very talented singer out of West Memphis, Arkansas. Not sure of her charges, but she has less than two months before going home. Readers pray that she will stay out of trouble and change her surrounding of people. She talks about her grandmother a lot. So, let's pray she will not disappoint Granny this time around. I've really had my way of touching some of these women lives so soon. If only these people would listen. It's all about a change that's much needed *now & later* in our troubled youth choices and decisions.

The ladies got up to go out to field squad to chop and pick vegetables. I have seen many on the back of a truck with a trailer connected to it. Some walked in their all white with hats on, some of the women cut grass and trimmed the edges around the prison. This prison would not be able to operate without us as prisoners. I understand those who participate in programs, because it can get them a time reduction of their sentence or work release. But, my sentence is sad, but true. It really makes me feel some type of way about the State of Arkansas. GOD will work it all out!

4:30 AM

I need some sleep now in order to continue my writing journey as a prisoner in Newport, Arkansas.

Chapter 15

Missy

8:30 AM

Loudness, bunks squeaking, and Missy has already been to pill call to do the exchange and she's high off plenty of pills. I laid on the bunk thinking about how she and Stephanie got into it with Yo-Yo last night over a transaction they did just two days ago.

One of Little Rock studs, Yo-Yo, is 5'5", 195 lbs., light-skinned, a gap in her teeth, short hair and hairy as a bear. She sent a message from Barrack 9, which is across the hallway, that they were short two Nutty Buddies, six envelopes, and Kool-Aid packs. She sent messages by Skittles saying they better make it right before she come and lay hands on somebody up in there.

Well, Skittles is the one who just snitched yesterday. She also had the payoff from commissary tucked in between her thighs sitting between her cotton panties and thermal. So, a gram of chocolate and peanut butter, a half ounce of Kool-Aid, a few cocaine white envelopes, and it's about to go down in Barrack 13. Yo-Yo wants to go nite-nite niggas!

Stephanie sent a message back to Yo-Yo saying. "You tell her I will make it right. All this time it hasn't been a problem. I gave her my word and I will make it right."

Missy, on the other hand stated. "You tell her not to be sending us no damn messages. If she hadn't missed pill call earlier, she would've gotten the rest of her payoff. We never cheated her. We make damn sure our end is right at all times and I can get other connections on pills around here."

Missy explained to me that she would never date a black man, but is weak for black studs. She has turned Stephanie into an educated trade and trafficking hood prisoner. Missy is also in love with Amberly, who has turned her away from ASU college studies to now studying LGBT.

Thumbs up for most of these programs that are in need of help and a change! Missy got into the SOFT program alright! Amber is a very cute "soft stud"... (LOL) She's enjoying the S.S.S. program alright! The sexy soft stud program and she may not ever make the parole board due to loving the same-sex.

Missy has been here for over ten years. She's serving time for killing her husband. They were both meth cookers and users. She will be eligible for parole in the next five years and is truly a character within herself.

Missy shared with me how she once lived for the tailgate parties with other Razorback fans and lived a very classy lifestyle. She married a good and hardworking business man with a family of three. Her husband later became abusive and they also started cooking meth and using it as well.

One night she tried to fight him off of her and pulled out a gun to defend herself. She aimed for his knees, but he fell on the couch and the aim of the gunshot went to his head and killed him. All for the love of meth!

On my first night moving into the wild Barrack 16, I thought it was the hole! With all the other noise, Missy stood over my head rocking the bunk with her MP4 player in her ears singing out loud "Black Panties" by R. Kelly and "You Ain't Hard" by T.I. To my left Kecia was making beats by banging on her bunk just as loud. My *lyfe"n"tyme* as a prisoner…Ugh!

Stephanie and Missy allowed me to listen to my favorite artist on their MP4 players. *"Darling Nicki"* and *"Diamond and Pearls"* by Prince. My sense of humor and personality got me the goodies not to mention, I'm a sexy soft stud too, all running concurrent …LOL.

To avoid trouble I kept it strictly on a cool level because of the drama I've witnessed which wasn't by far a surprise to me. As the leader of the black gay community, I repeatedly listened to Mary J Blige's *"No More Drama"*.

I always made it clear to these women in prison and even outside of this place that I've had my share of ups and downs with my wife, but she's my choice of a woman. This has become both of our journey and I wasn't going to break her heart again. It takes a strong woman to deal with me and my *lyfe"n"tyme and* AngieSaidThat!

Chapter 16

Sergeant Ox...Ugh!

Does GOD always answer prayer? We can be confident in GOD's response to our prayers if we submit first to his will. Three different times I begged the Lord to take it away and each time he said. *"My power works best in your weakness."*

Sometimes, like my brother Paul, a repeated prisoner, we find that GOD answers prayers by giving us not what we ask for, but something better. I enjoy reading scriptures from the Bible, from the New Testament, Proverbs, and Psalms. They feed my spirit and make me feel so good! My spirit remained humble even in the midst of the devil being all around this compound.

Again, Sgt. Ox yelled. "When I say count time and you see the red light, don't get off your bunk! I mean don't get up until after count or I'm going to write you up!"

She reminded me so much of Sgt. Gib at 3910 W. Roosevelt County Jail in Little Rock. She was always stating, "My desk. My unit. My trash bags. My. My. My!" The sad part is if these guards were ever out of a job they wouldn't amount to anything. My, my, my goodness!

A crispy blue uniform with a small pin on the upper part of their shirt does not give anybody the right to mistreat GOD's children. Sgt. Ox is truly a ghetto authorized black woman in her mind. She really thinks it's all about her. People kill me getting certain positions and allowing their jobs and a little authority to go to their heads. They seem to have forgotten the history of our people which cannot be taken away, and most of the time it is our very own black people that have forgotten where they came from. We rather be divided versus sticking together. So many lawsuits could have been filed, but who am I to take a stand.

Behind me would be every color, but my own. Our hair is a problem in this prison to be natural. Are you kidding me?

It reminds me so much of my black gay community. I have always been the one to stand up because my black LGBT people didn't have anywhere safe to go without there being complaints and there were no awareness programs.

Many programs claimed to care on Facebook or with falsified public paperwork they have presented to the media to look good. No different than most of the ones running for election. To look up and see our former governor on commercials, but they can't even donate a paper to our black college? UGH! Will it be me, AngieSaidThat, donating my series of books to our historical black colleges and community colleges? The books of my prison *lyfe "n" tyme* about me trying to understand our American politics and how bills are passed.

I got Stephanie's, the ASU graduate student, MP4 player to listen to *"Diamonds and Pearls"*. To be honest I wanted to listen to the choices of music of a smart white teacher with a bachelor's degree and two master's degrees. I wanted to know what her musical taste was like, the daughter of the top of the line BMW (black man wish) salesman. I've even owned a BMW myself, but after a few problems with them the name becomes "bring money witcha" and AngieSaidThat!

I strolled down her music feeds and surprisingly the very first songs on her playlist were *"Real Life Fantasy"* by JaRule, *"Don't You Wanna Stay"* by Kelly Clarkson, *"Ours"* by Taylor Swift, and

"Erotica" by Madonna. She truly had numerous of songs to listen to and was no doubt a big fan of JaRule, Usher and T.I. I must say, please don't judge a book by the cover. It's important to read what's inside. To judge our American people by the color of one's skin, same-sex preference, community upbringing, occupation, or education is an injustice. You never know the inside of one's mind.

It's all about the college kids in our state, and we as blacks have it the hardest on education. Our history can't be talked down or taken away! And if our American people are focused just on education then truly our lawmakers should be supportive of our youth in all the surrounding areas. Where is the equality and fairness that involves all of today's issues? Angiesaidthat!

Studies shows a congressional committee might ask the American Association for the Advancement of Science for help in drafting a complex ProVision Biotechnology, meaning exploration of biological processes in industry and medicine. A court might learn more about how the college admission process really works by reading a brief submitted respectfully by the American Association of Colleges. Material that interests groups prepare for our government and it is quite detailed. And let's talk about our community with the public and you. We need interested groups to try to influence our government by using press releases and background briefings in the newspaper media, appearances on our radio programs, FM and AM radio stations, and T.V. news shows. We need broadcasting advertising. They need to offer the most important and factual information to replace the misleading and false information. Those who have grown up in my neighborhood simply call it what it is, a lie. No ifs, ands, or butts about it. Let's talk about the truth.

We need what most of our American taxpayers don't know about in today's, tomorrow, weekly, monthly, and yearly issues. It's true of course, no government is perfect, but a democracy should at least try to live up to their standards and be willing to acknowledge its shortcomings. Congress too has become so increasingly specialized that laws and policies are made by committees and subcommittees that take on a similar focus although bias. Our government has become extremely responsive to small pressure groups, but very unresponsive to people of a large crowd and races, the homosexuals in our community. My final word, sad but true. Politics is not all serious business. Both politicians and their politics are somewhat just as funny as myself and I've then told laughter is therapeutic to one's mind and soul.

No disrespect to our government, but the truth has no defense. Allow me to write and give my papers to our community. If anyone from our state outside of a Clinton have it in their vision to ever run for presidency, you need to change the outdated ways of thinking and upgrade the same as the latest new iPhone. We as people must stand for something or we will fall for anything. To have sentence me to twenty-one unjustified years is an injustice, and just imagine those who can't read. What if you take the blame for your younger sisters? This is no longer a nightmare about 12-12- 12.

I've woke up in dusty blues at 3201 W. Roosevelt County Jail and now currently in all white in the state prison in Newport, Arkansas, and all over a gap in my teeth in my *lyfe"n"tyme* trying to help our community.

It would be awesome if our lawmakers formed interest groups to visit behind these white walls about the unfair justice, the overbite of sentencing, 70% laws and etc.

I looked at the time and it was 8:30 PM in Barrack 13. I can't stop thinking about A.D. reminds me so much of the actor Omar Epps, who played in many movies and one of my favorites, *"Love and Basketball"*.

While I was writing she walked over to my table and stated. "I'm about to go on suicide watch. Once I find out for sure if my sister Jackie is no longer at Wrightsville prison. She's still showing up in the system. I had someone to check and I want to be with my sister. She's due to have her baby there."

I felt helpless looking up and listening. I tried to comfort her. "I know how it feels Lil' Bro, wanting to be with your sisters and nieces. I miss my twin nieces with all my heart. As long as you're okay, why are you going on suicide watch?" I asked.

"See, if I find out she's already released, I won't be able to go there, but if she's there I'm leaving here." She replied.

"Okay, cool!" I smiled as I tuned into listening to Anthony Hamilton's, *"Never Love Again"*. I decided to stop writing and line up for rec time and do some sit-ups. I needed to release some aches and pains by working out all the tension.

I looked around stilled tuned into music on Stephanie's MP4 player. She expressed to me how Usher is the man of her dreams, *"Yeah!"* I thought to myself she should've gotten probation for having sex with a sexually active seventeen year old and I disagree with her education position causing a difference in her verdict.

However, honey if an educated white ASU graduate from Lonoke, Arkansas married Usher and the KKK got a hold of this news, surely we all know what they would do to Usher's music career! *"Let It Burn!"* All music would be donated to ASU… LOL AngieSaidThat!

Instantly, I thought of one of our educated black men, Tracy Steele, who last year ran for Mayor of North Little Rock, and the statements made against his longtime friend and police officer, Tommy Norman, for campaigning in police uniform for Mr. Steele. Just vision yourself being in Hot Springs at Oaklawn Park. The horses are racing neck to neck, the crowd is drinking, loud noise, and you are nervous in need of a win. We do not know how much money has been wagered on some of these horses, but we are praying for the right one to win. The jockeys' whip the horses necks to run a close race.

The number two horse, Steele, is in the lead. The number one horse, Smith, is nose to nose. The number two horse nose is down and the number one horse nose is looking up at the finish line, but it confuses the crowd as to who really won the race. It's a runoff!

An instant replay just the same as the race of our North Little Rock Mayor's Office. Our people didn't get out and vote again. Look at their tickets and the favorite was the second horse. It was just too many odds against Steele. The winner is Joe Smith for the mayor of North Little Rock City.

I must share this. If our people stop judging and quit trying to give the American people false hope and just keep it real, they would admit that their lawmakers are so against our LGBT community, which makes up a great percentage of our communities and votes. We matter! And do you people know that President Obama is a smart man? He supports LGBT equal rights and he respects us. He doesn't allow judgment to divide our race, gender, religion and foolishness. He loves as GOD say. None of you have to go home with any of us. What's wrong with allowing us to love one another and enjoy our home and life with the one we love whether it's black, white, same-sex, handicap and even as a prisoner? I stand for equality. None of you can do what the Almighty is capable of doing.

As bad as some of you think that it's a spirit, a phase, or the devil, and to witness a preacher man standing in front of Chick-Fil-A restaurant last year holding two extension cord ends together protesting that GOD made Adam and Eve, not Adam and Steve. He placed the two ends of the plugs together screaming, "You can't get this to connect."

But what he didn't know in my R. Kelly voice is, *"I don't see nothing with a little bump and grind."* We stood out there with posters and signs protecting our rights for equality.

Too many of our politicians try their best to convince the public through the media and campaign advertisements on issues many want to hear just to get their votes. Let's try keeping it real with our American people and see the long lines formed with people wanting to cast their votes for those running for these positions.

Shortly after working out and thinking about my *lyfe"n"tyme,* I found myself laughing about those wanting to be in my books. Returning back to Barrack 13, an inmate name Pace walked up to me as we lined up at rec time.

"Angie, am I still in your book?" She asked with excitement and smiling.

"Yes, Boo. I got you!" I replied laughing.

"Look, me and Crystal had sex last night in the shower and she used the toy on me. Afterward I had to suck it." She said laughing.

"What are you talking about?" I asked.

"We made a dildo with a hair comb. We wrapped it with toilet tissue and placed a plastic glove and then a rubber glove on it. And it feels so good." She explained laughing.

In my friend, Frank Whitmore's voice, "Are you kidding me?" I said killing myself laughing. "So, you wanted to suck it and tell me about it? I asked. Thinking about the materials needed to make this penis in prison and now I see the reasons for the yeast infections and yellow panties.

"Angie, you know when it's been in you and the mood takes you there. You know what I'm talking about." She is laughing.

"Well, sweetheart this is my first time in Newport prison, and I promise I will not be trying any of it. Trust me!" I told her.

I laughed assuring her that it would be in the book and before I could get out the rec area, King of Avenue, a stud from Little Rock, and Charm, who is also known as Brandy, was laughing and talking about how she performed oral sex on Charm. She inserted her thumb inside her butt. I've heard that plenty of times, but everybody wants it to be in my book, which causes me to jump from one thing to the next on different subjects.

I'm kindly asking my readers to follow me and stay connected. I am in prison and what I'm trying to do is allow your mind to be behind these walls with me. I also want to let parents know how important it is to talk to your children and watch their surroundings, and also let people know this is not a place anyone wants to be *now or later*.

I can't sugar coat what I am experiencing by any means as a prisoner. I have to keep it real with my readers. We all have plenty of thoughts and ideas racing through our minds from watching movies and reading newspaper, but I'm here living in Newport Prison with the reality of my *lyfe"n"tyme*.

Chapter 17

With GOD, I'm Free!

Friday   9/26/2014   6:50 AM

"Line up for the safety meeting!" The officer screamed.

I jumped up in my state provided thermals, my commissary t-shirt, and a sweat shirt that Missy advised me to put on to stay warm. Unable to brush my teeth and rushing because it is truly a write up if you're not in the gym listening to a prisoner read the rules of the safety guidelines and have us sign off. Returning back to Barrack 13, we ain't learned nothing about safety. It's all about our signatures on these documents to continue grant funding.

I came back to brush my teeth and wash my face. Others went back to sleep and I needed to write in peace. I thought about Dr. Hearne on Wright Avenue telling me to have a vegetable blended drink for breakfast. Due to my imprisonment it's a limited amount of healthy choices in prison. I got a package of crushed vegetables, the seasoning from my cream of chicken noodles, and chopped onion seasoning and made the closest I could to a cup of healthy vegetable soup. I also had an apple fruit bar. Shout-out to Dr. Hearne from Newport Prison!

While sitting at the table writing after count time listening to *"Open My Heart"* by Yolanda Adams with the volume turned up, I allowed this song to enter into every part of my body. My tearful eyes continued to blink as I sipped my tea thinking about last night. I finally got two more visitations approved by the deputy warden. Both are dated 9/23/14.

First, Sharon Smith, sister, phone and visitations approved.

Second, LaShay Watkins, sister, phone and visitations approved.

My third piece of paper stated $5.30 off my account, which meant my book was mailed off to my sister, Kim, along with a copy of my Rule 37 Appeal that I needed her to forward to my wife.

As the music continued to play, *"Lord, talk to me. Alone in a room. It's just me and you. I feel so lost I don't know what to do, but what if I choose the wrong thing to do? My mind feels so cloudy. Guide me until I'm sure. My hope and dreams are fading fast. I'm crying out to you. You're the only one to pull me through. Open up my heart."*

The lyrics had me feeling some type of way, but I knew in my heart, the *Lord's will* would be done. I just needed his guidance. I wanted him and needed him to guide me. I just need to hear a single word. Just one word made a difference in my case. A text message from my friend, Vona Cox, made a change in my *lyfe"n"tyme* with GOD, and none of this would've been possible without searching for my purpose in *lyfe"n"tyme*.

I looked over at A.D. during count time as she packed on 9/26/14 in the early morning hours to go to Wrightsville. To see a young black stud with her voice and personality behind these white walls walking behind a yellow line and unable to shop commissary was sad to me. To witness Missy and Stephanie give her soap, deodorant, and snacks items really made me write, write, write, and continue to write. I didn't want to line up for chow and prayed for mercy on my appeal to be granted. I noticed snot running from my nose and I held back my tears, but the tears were actually coming from my nose. I wiped my nose with my hand, not wanting to stop writing and get any of the thin state provided toilet tissue. I started pressing down even harder on my paper. The volume vibration blasted through my body, mind, and soul playing *"One Wing"* by Jordan Sparks. The sniffles and snot from my nose felt as if I had overdosed on cocaine or was in a Chicago snow storm without any clothes on.

I went from sniffling to anger to hurt over A.D.'s struggle. The fact that she has been in and out of jail since she was fifteen years old made me feel some kind of way. I had to get up and use some tissue anyway. I walked over to bunk 33, my assigned area and placed my right hand on Missy's back to easily slide around her as she put on her commissary make-up. I grabbed the tissue and went to the mirror to blow my nose. No signs of a cold, but the gospel will take you there with words of the truth. This time I'm not referring to the races. *"His eyes is on the sparrow and I know he watches me", a*s the lyrics says. My heart beats increased and I envisioned programs for the LGBT youth.

My readers and people may very well think that because I'm in prison now that there is no way the community will listen to me, but I'm free! I didn't feel this good all over in the free world, even with putting on my events, as I do right now in all white writing about my *lyfe"n"tyme.* Most will not understand it, thinking I had it made with my cars, women, being a club owner, and a comedian, but I was missing someone. I was missing GOD! He quickly gave what many call life! I thought I had it all, but in less than seconds I lost it all. I didn't have purpose in my *lyfe"n"tyme.*

The thought of those who think they have it all and not fulfilling God's purpose in their life is sad to me now. Trust me, I've lived it, seen it, talked about it, buried it, serving time for it, and now writing about it! Do you people know David in the book of Psalms 103:14–17? He understands how we are. He knows we are only dust and our days on earth are like grass. Like wildflowers, we bloom and die. The wind blows and we are gone as though we have never been here.

But, the love of the Lord remains forever with those who fear him. As for me, I will continue to praise him *now & later* and I will fear no evil. I want to stand before our lawmakers in Washington and our newly elected officials and speak about the injustice of our laws. I don't care if it's John, Mike, Mark, Asa, Tom or even Ugly Mike on 12th Street. We need changes in our state! AngieSaidThat

Yes, I am in prison, but does it sound as if I'm a criminal? My Facebook page doesn't give out false information about AngieSaidThat events. My heart is hurting in prison over facts of injustice, unfairness and inequality. To even see the youth of our black gay community endure racist acts in this prison on a daily basis is heartbreaking. No one can force their religion in one's spirit to receive good time on these programs. Do you not know most sign up only to get out and go home? Most are back in less than one to five months on drugs charges. Repeatedly! Some of these federal taxpayer programs are not working people! Let's tell the truth and enlighten the public.

So, are some of these programs even worth our taxpayers' money? Hell no, that's why the Chaplain here at Newport played a smart Christian game to steal money and caused a scandal. He was able to help free his secret prison lover after ten years walking behind this yellow line, count time, chow time, and Christian time. She's free from Newport Prison, but what about fulfilling GOD's Purpose? The Chaplain allowed his flesh to become weakened. He wanted to taste the fruit the same as Eve did in the garden, but it's a price to pay behind it. None of us can hide from GOD at the end of the day. No! I wasn't joining the Christian programs here. They are hard on us as homosexuals, but are mad when we enjoy a bowl of the female forbidden fruit loop! People hate the truth of facts. Hypocrites!

I remember my attorney, Stanley, telling me he didn't see any gaps in my case, but I was able to prove facts on not just the gap in my teeth. I also know that he's great friends with the judge on my case and the many horses he told me that were out of the barn. Well, GOD created us all and one thing I do know is he will reveal all of them at some point in our lives. Many will return back to dust and be judged by GOD's authority. I'm just letting people know to be careful who you vote for. Look for truth, not advertisement. If I tell you to place your money on the one horse to win and the two horse to place, and the three horse to show, do it and get your winning ticket ready to cash in at the I.R.S. window at the end of the race. I study the facts now!

They get paid regardless, and yes my appointed counsel needed to protect her job and I can't say I blame her as she rushed to pump her breast for her first newborn baby girl feedings in the midst of my trial.

They made me out to be a monster and lied like we planned this at my club. One witness, Jo-Jo, and the co-conspirator, Marty, court records reveal they both said two different areas in the club. This discussion never took place in my club. Marty' hidden background record speaks for itself on guns and robberies. However, due to the fact of my other series of books, I will not entertain my readers with the past when the Bible speaks of the truth. GOD knows my heart and forgiveness is written all over June 4, 2014 in this judge court room.

But, until justice is fairly served, my name behind these bars will remain open to the American readers informing them that our state lawmakers need to be reformed and what is hidden from the public. Someone will eventually listen to me regardless if it's *now & later!* AngeiSaidThat

In Psalm 7:1-5, my big brother David says, *"I come to you for protection, O Lord. My GOD, save me from my prosecutors. Rescue me! If you don't they will maul me like a lion tearing me to pieces with no one to rescue me; O Lord, My GOD, if I have done wrong or am guilty of injustice, if I have betrayed a friend or plundered my enemy without cause, then let my enemies capture me; let them trample me into the ground, let my honor be left in the dust."*

The prosecutor said I sent Marty money in jail so he would remain quiet. No, the truth of the matter was his mother was off work sick and unable to send him money. I sent him $50.00 in the midst of her illness because that's just my heart. Not hush money! Surely she's smart enough to know that. Even Warden Frances' youngest daughter knows FIFTY DOLLARS isn't hush money. She surely convinced the jury of twelve people who are just registered voters without any expertise if the law. She convinced them on hearsay and gossip. There was no evidence of me having a gun or any prior felonies, but yet I am convicted because I have a gap in my teeth and sentenced to twenty-one unjustified years in prison. A conviction of the gap in my lyfe"n"tyme off of hearsay! Voters, is this justice in our state?

11:30 AM

Most are up thanking GOD that it's Friday and they just got paid. The thoughts of my friend, Shirley Martin, crossed my mind which made me smile as I was writing. The thought of her calling me "Angeline" and telling me, "Girl, you are too much!" She works for the State at the Health Department. She is a very sweet and caring person. I can clearly vision her reading my books. The truth has no defense and the truth is what has made my name, AngieSaidThat, so well known throughout our state, the cities of Memphis, Dallas and other surrounding areas. My creations are not by far a mistake, just pick up your phone and call *"Heaven Sent"*.

It wasn't by far a mistake that GOD wanted me to visit prison just as Joseph, Silas, Timothy, and Paul. Now, as far Paul, he is what the system calls a habitual criminal… LOL. I'm more like my brother, Silas, who experienced prison and freed himself through the faith of our Creator in Jesus name.

I'm truly representing my Father. Without a doubt we sometimes forget the fact that GOD's people are everywhere. Yes, we have some devilment injected into our spirits everywhere, inside and outside these white walls. We never know about the people next-door or even laying in the bed with us and we think we know them inside and out!

A few days later I picked up Meaka's written fourth step and read it. You just never know! That is why it's so important to pray for healing, strength, guidance, and protection from GOD. We must pray for GOD to keep his arms wrapped around our family, friends, and even a dosage for our enemies. We need to praise him daily, weekly, monthly, and yearly. My calendar is filled with GOD in my *lyfe "n" tyme*.

Chapter 18

The Demon Auntie

I must share with my readers what a *"Drunk in Love"* will do, but unlike Beyonce and Jay Z, as I continue to share Meaka's story.

My uncle had completely lost it before he died; he went over to the next door neighbor's house dressed in a long leather coat. He was naked and when the cops arrived he flashed the police officer. At this time I had started running the streets, selling dope, and trying to take care of myself. My uncle wouldn't come to look for me anymore. He lost himself before he passed although he took my advice to leave me alone. The front of his head with a symbol of a pitch fork. He later got sentenced a year in jail and was voted out the neighborhood. My aunt took advantage of people in bad situations and ten children in the same house got SSI checks. Social security income. She moved another man into the house and had no choice but to send him back to Biscoe, Arkansas, after my uncle was released from jail. She left my uncle home by himself while she took trips to see her boyfriend. One time my uncle was trying to get her attention as she pulled out the driveway, claiming again, she was going to the store to get coffee. By the time she got back the ambulance was there at the house and my uncle was D.O.A. (Dead on Arrival). To tell this story gets me emotional.

My granny would say something to him, but it did no good. I remember my grandma crying and asking him. "Little boy why ya' want with this woman? She ain't no good!"

He just kept right on bathing my grandmother ignoring her question. I had to clean and bath my grandma because his wife was scared to touch her. My uncle did anything to keep the flow of money coming in to please his wife. Including getting over on the government, setting up appointment in order for us children to go and play crazy so that they could get disability checks in our names. Insurance fraud suits started kicking in and government lawsuits. They started living like George and Weezy from "The Jefferson's" and moving on up.

One day my aunt and uncle plotted an accident against The Central Arkansas Transit Bus Company in Little Rock to file a false insurance claim. They planned for her to get on the bus holding me and when the bus started moving she was to fall with me. And that's exactly how it went down! They had a vehicle parked around the corner waiting on them. My aunt was holding me and when she fell with me there were knots all over my head. I was actually hurt. They took me to the hospital as well as her, and then back home they sat around the table filing a claim. They pulled the same stunt in stores with the other children. I would take it all in and I started doing my own stunts. There was no stopping us. We burned down houses we lived in and filed insurance claims.

My uncle started using cocaine and drinking, and I have never gotten over that lady. My uncle loved her more than his family. She is always on my mind. Even after leaving her house, she affected me a great deal. I find myself in tears about the treatment I received from her. How could someone be so evil to a child? She never loved me and she made sure I knew it. I feel as if I can't wait for her to die, so I can spit on her grave. I know that isn't a good thought for me, because wishing death upon her could truly happen to me first. Every time something goes wrong in my life I can't keep allowing my past to haunt me. I gotta get rid of my nightmares or I will never have a peace of mind. I have to let go and let GOD. I'm truly learning the real concept of letting go and let God. My aunt would never allow someone to treat her biological children like she treated us. She would die and go to hell over her own. I couldn't understand how my own mama could choke me, spit tobacco in my face, curse me out and hit me with objects.

I would always end up at Mr. Bob's house. The other old man that would fix my zipper, but Mr. Bob showed me attention and fed me because Lord knows I would be so hungry, dusty, and tired. He showed me kindness. My aunt went to Biscoe to gamble and hang out at a hole in the wall. She also loved the fortune tellers. She'd be wanting to know if she was gonna be rich. Everything was about money, power, and control with her.

I remember her jumping on my mama, she busted my mama's lip and punched her in the face several times. She knew my mama had a problem and couldn't help it. She knew my mama couldn't defend herself. I also remember when she was punching and kicking my great-aunt Maria because she got up and told everybody in church how she was scared for her life. How she thought they were going to kill her. It took my uncle and aunt by surprise. They weren't expecting that I was kinda shocked myself. I thought she was gonna sing a song, but she told everything they were doing to her. Every time I would run away to be with my siblings my great-aunt would find out where I was hiding in the house and make me leave. Well, when my uncle talked her into leaving me with him for a day or two she never returned to her home and she finally got a chance to see what I was going through. My great-aunt Maria started begging for me to please take her away from there and also telling me I could stay with her. She did make it to the nursing home, unlike my grandma who suffered in her own home.

My uncle never said nothing about the complaints my granny had. Oh, back to when my great-aunt was at the church. After she got up telling how she was treated, they loaded us up in the car and were also trying to hurry up and get my auntie in the car. She had embarrassed the hell out of them. As she was getting in the car my uncle's wife was punching her all in the head and kicking her. My auntie was crying. When my uncle came out of the church we drove off packed like sardines. I felt like my uncle should have been ashamed of himself for allowing her to get away with all she was doing. He had no control over his wife. My auntie called the police a few times, but they convinced the cops she was senile. My auntie and granny both sang the same song while being a residence of the Hunt's house. "Take me home, I want to go home." They'll be yelling, crying, and pleading with my uncle.

My granny laid helpless. She suffered from some sickness and wanted to rush her death. My uncle's wife's daughter, Tenise, use to go in there and bite my granny toes. My grandma couldn't move, but she would cry for someone to come help her. My uncle's wife would be standing there peeking behind the door laughing. Her nephew and daughter would throw shoes at her and provoke my granny. She would go over her sister Dee's house to gamble playing pity-pat. She also had a candy store inside her home.

On a daily basis I was being punched and scratched by her children. My uncle wasn't allowed to whip her children. My aunt kept me looking bad. She dressed her kids decent and I was always filthy and nappy headed. I had to search for me something to wear. Most times it would be my uncle's pants with a string tied around the waist. The children made fun of me at school. I couldn't focus on my schoolwork because I was too busy being a class clown in order to keep them from laughing at me personally. But they would still laugh at my clothes so I acted out because I was angry from the problems at home. This was public school which was too busy dealing with my behavior problems to teach me. They would just throw me in the quiet room and shut the door leaving me yelling and cursing.

My aunt broke me down by calling me ugly, stinky, telling me my mama didn't want me, and my uncle never wanted me either. She said she had to make my uncle take me in. She'd pat her butt and vagina at me telling me to kiss it. She would say. "Kiss my pussy or kiss my ass bitch!"

One day my aunt loaded me and some of their children into the vehicle together. She had me to sit in the front seat which I found odd. She never put me in the front seat before her biological children. We were on the freeway getting off onto another exit as if we were headed towards Children's Hospital, when she decided to push me out of the moving vehicle. My face was disfigured and bleeding. She took me home, instead of taking me to the hospital. My uncle asked what happened to my face and she told him I fell out the car. I never told him what happened.

I never understood why she hated me so much. If my uncle would give me food that was left over from his meal she would take it saying, "We don't show differences around here."

One day we all went into Harvest Foods Grocery Store before taking a road trip to Biscoe, Arkansas. My aunt bought her daughter a package of Hubba Bubba bubble gum and didn't buy me any. I told my uncle and she overheard me telling him. Once everybody had loaded back into the vehicle except me, I was the last one to get in. As I was getting in she began kicking me extremely hard with her high heeled boot. I didn't say anything, I just looked at her with tears filled in my eyes. She thought my uncle would love me more than her children.

Her children told everybody that I played with myself with broken glass causing my vagina to bleed. They also lied and said I was sleeping with my brother. They did and said anything to degrade me in front of others. Growing up she never bought me any personal hygiene items. Every time people came over they called me nasty, stanking, musty, and all kinds of names. You name it and they called me it. I slept where I could find a place to sleep, but her children had no problems. They had bedrooms with dressers and televisions in their room. If I was lucky I might get to watch some television.

Chapter 19

All My Life I Had To Fight

I always had to fight. Almost every day I had to fight one of her children. It didn't matter, girls or boys, I had to fight. She did nothing about them punching me, scratching my face up with really, really bad deep scratches. Her oldest daughter would always target my face. At times when my aunt and uncle left home, the oldest seem like she would be lying in the cut like a snake waiting for them to leave. She would be waiting to attack me. To this day I think everyone is out to get me. I've made bad choices and I've committed many crimes based on scheming and hustling. I was exposed to it. I grew up thinking you make ends meet by any means necessary.

But, I also learned some good things from the way they mistreated me and others. I learned not to do something to someone else that you wouldn't want done to you. Especially not to hurt old people. Today, I love old people and I'm very compassionate towards them. I love children. I didn't mistreat my man because I witnessed my uncle's life.

I remember one time my aunt burned down our house when there was snow on the ground. We had to run out of the house. I had no shoes on standing there in the snow shaking to death and looking at the house going up in flames. The Red Cross came out there and put us in a hotel. You know the rest. They contacted the insurance company and later collected money for the house and the merchandise the house contained. This happened three different times with our homes.

Today, I'm trying to find myself thinking they played a big part in screwing up my life. All the abuse, lies, stealing, cheating, scams, alcohol, and jokes has taken its toll on me. Later I was once in a program in Pine Bluff, Arkansas, and met this guy who I really liked. His name was Tony. We were in the same program and went to the same school. He wrote me all the time. I felt like he really cared for me. He encouraged me to stay in school. No one had ever shown me that type of love or attention. His foster mom, Rose, called and asked to bring him over to see me. My aunt agreed, but later said I was too young to have a boyfriend and I never saw or heard from him again. I still wonder what ever happened to him. I will never in this lifetime understand my uncle's demonic wife.

Chapter 20

Little Rock Finest Entertainers

I tuned into Monique's MP4 player listening to the lyrics, *"Good Love Will Make You Cry"* by Carl Marshall while eating on a commissary honey bun and sipping water. At 4:50 PM the officer yelled. "Chow-time!" I couldn't stop writing long enough for anything but to use the restroom, get some water, and a bite to eat.

Quickly taking the noodles, pizza sauce, pepperoni, block cheese, vegetables, chopped onions and jalapeno peppers I created my commissary no-bake spaghetti dish. I slid my tongue across my teeth and licked my lips because it was so delicious. I tuned in listening to smooth jazz thinking about one of Little Rock's finest, Mr. Rodney Block and my first time ever seeing him play at Club Trois on Asher Avenue. The best performance of Little Rock jazz artists yet! I was also thinking back on our community's love that night at a fundraiser for one of our local DJ's. DJ No Name was battling for his life trying to beat cancer.

After I finished with a few minutes of comedy by AngieSaidThat, Rodney Block looked at me smiling. He's 5'9", 160 pounds, dressed to impress, brown eyes, pretty teeth, nice clean cut, and dimples.

"Hey, you are bad on that microphone!" He said laughing.

"Thanks, Boo, but not nearly as bad as you are with the piece of instrument Bro." I replied and we both laughed.

It is my vision and mission to get myself from behind these white walls and to have Rodney play at my book signing. It's just a matter of *lyfe"n"tyme*. True enough, I came in contact with a lot of Arkansas great and talented artists who I still allow to cross my mind.

Talents such as Dell Smith, Gatewood, Keith Salvage, Dino Davis, LaTrisha Rucker, Kim Pettis, DD, Cat Daddy, Chantel Williams, Kesha Rashad, and I got to give a huge shout-out to William Staggers due to the fact last year on Valentine's Day, I surprised my wife at her job with a sing-a-gram. He sung *"Let's Stay Together"* by Al Green. William did his thing! You would be surprise at what the heart can do with the smallest amount of money. The meaning alone feels like a new car to most if it comes from the heart.

That's what the prosecutor argued. I needed money on 12-12-12 for my wife, my lover's birthday. Mrs. Prosecutor, a beautiful woman herself, convinced the jury into believing that. In fact, she was so sure that she held up a picture to the twelve jurors. A random picture of another woman, name Valerie Williams, sitting with me at my club. The truth was, Valerie Williams worked for me at the club, but the prosecutor claimed I threw my lover, Valerie Perry, a birthday party. Another lie presented as evidence. This is what registered voters do without any expertise of the law, they believe whatever is presented to them, facts or not.

They were not a jury of my peers, one was dozing off, and one was discussing the case outside the courtroom in the hallways. The twelve of them looked at a picture with another black woman by the name of Valerie sitting next to me at a birthday party that was fabricated by the prosecutor. The gap in my teeth has me currently facing twenty-one unjustified years in prison. How fair are our American voters and the justice system?

Chapter 21

Open My Heart

The 15th Amendment guaranteed that the right to vote could not be denied or abridged on the basis of race. It was ratified in 1870 and the promise of the 15th Amendment wasn't fully realized for almost another century.

The 14th Amendment was clearly intended to make it illegal for any state or government to treat African Americans as second-class citizens. The amendment addresses citizenship rights and equal protection of the laws, and was proposed in response to issues related to former slaves following the American Civil War.

These laws that once deprived the blacks of many basic rights including the right to testify in court, make contracts, travel, speak freely, and peaceably assemble. Some believed that the amendments would simply ban discrimination based on race.

This is why my case will call for higher judicial standards. Being black and gay damn near got me life. Twenty-one unjustified years in my *lyfe "n" tyme*. When the government classifies on the basis of race or religion its action raise immediate suspicions of illegal discrimination. It's known as strict scrutiny. True enough, they had black jurors on my case but same as the white jurors, they were biased and prejudiced against homosexuality in our Christian state of Arkansas.

Our state fails to realize that a great percentage of our community our LGBT people play a high tech and important role with everything we do on a daily basis. Most may think as a lesbian that I'm just talking out the side of my neck, but listen as far as the state of Arkansas is concerned I enjoy our state. My mother's foundation is here. I'm so past their outdated judgmental ways of thinking. Do you all think it's a game? An example of facts; GOD allowed a black president not once, but twice to be elected in the United States. You all need to be reminded of this truth. This is GOD's earth and all his creations. We are all on borrowed *lyfe"n"tyme*. Although states can encourage change and social progress, they can also lead to waste. Most voters are mad because President Obama wants to raise wages, but the states have little idea on how much a job is really worth. I've been told right now most only people are eating lunch. Who determines when it's dinner time people?

Yes, I know my books will have plenty of lawmaker critics, Newport Prison critics, and American critics. Oh well, new ideas deserve critical arguments and discussions. Blame it on GOD. I'm just living up to a text message from my friend Vona R. Cox, asking what is my purpose in life? My reply, AngieSaidThat in Jesus name!

I looked up at the time as the guard called on this Friday, the 26 of September, for all the prisoners in Barrack 13 to line up for Rec time as the clock struck 7:00 PM. I placed the MP4 on repeat to continue writing and listening over and over again to Yolanda Adams song, *"Open My Heart."*

A citizen in a single year may be expected to vote in city, county, school district, statewide, and federal elections. People, do you as voters follow the true actions of the City Council, the County, the school board, the state legislator, and the Congress? Well, please add the Mayor, the Governor, the President, and not to mention the court systems. It may be overwhelming to everyone. How do people such as myself governor over sharp attacks on justice unfairly served. Yes, it truly hurts that I'm currently unable to vote, but I'm putting up a fight just like Rosa Parks. She continued to go back to the clerk's office until she was able to vote and she refused to give up her seat on the bus.   We can't talk down on our black history and it can't be taken away from us.

Chapter 22

Prisoner Favoritism

"Mail call!" The officer yelled.

I stopped writing to listen for my name to be called. The last to be called at the ending of it.

"Richardson!"

An e-mail sent on September 25, 2014 @ 10:56 PM. I tuned into the song, *"Made to Love You"* by Gerald Levert.

Email:

From: Valerie Perry

Sent: September 25, 2014   10:56 PM

Subject: Hello Baby

Hello Baby. How are you? I got your letters today. I'm not going to even comment on the one. Just SMH... so spoiled! LaShay said she is still waiting to get approved which you need to check on because she should be approved by now. Neika is back and she has taken over typing for me since she has nothing else to do until she finds a job. I hope you are not letting that place, women, or people get to you. I didn't want you to move, but it might be a good idea especially since you are already having problems so early. I was reading some of the prison rights and stuff and they had something in there about homosexuality and harassment! I will get some more facts for you and see if you have other options. I called down there and I have not gotten a return call yet. LaShay also said she called to and no one has returned her call yet either. We are counting down the days to come see you in 20 days. I'm going to print and mail you the article on the bust involving OG because it's so much to send in an email. I love you, miss you. Please stay strong.

8:30 PM

I got out of the shower and started writing my wife a sweet and meaningful letter. I had to express how I really loved and appreciate her through it all. I admit I am spoiled. She knows me like a book. I'm so thankful that her only daughter, Neika, is back home to type my book. By all means with her great typing skills it should not take over three weeks to have it typed up and ready for the editor.

Now what puzzled me is that I haven't heard from Kim as of today. This is what frightens me. She's working on "*12-12-12: The Cries Behind The Bars*". My mind races between the election time and getting my books out to enlighten the public.

I am unable to make any calls due to my restrictions. What kills me is that the state laws are so much different than the federal laws. To place prisoners on restriction over petty D.R.'s and unable to call or visit their love ones over small mistakes such as your hair in twists, or having naturally curly hair, or dreads is stupid!

A white inmate steals my envelopes and I'm in trouble, but the Major throws Missy's D.R. out and she gets to shop commissary. I get to window shop Little Debbie, unlike Missy, who is eating coochie in the showers as the officer's D.R. paperwork stated. "I heard the slur sound with two inmates in the shower."

Really? But, this is my *lyfe"n"tyme* now as a prisoner in Newport, Arkansas. Ugh!

Chapter 23

Hearsay

After taking a break and thinking, I tuned into the election candidates, I had a newspaper article placed in my face. I looked over to my left as a young lady who knew of me outside of these bars made sure I got the newspaper. It reads Friday, September 26, 2014. I found it funny that I've just written earlier about this year's election, politics, politicians, and to see this in the paper. Asa Hutchinson said let program work and Ross says expand Pre-K. It splits the governor's race.

Two main parties' governor candidates for Arkansas, Mike Ross and Asa Hutchinson, were debating at the Grand Hotel in Fayetteville. Democratic Mike wants to fully fund Pre-kindergarten for families making up to a percentage of the poverty level or $59,374.00 for a family of three. Republican Asa says it's too soon to consider an expansion speaking to a crowd of 190 at a meeting at The Political Animals Club of Northwest Arkansas.

Asa said Mike effectively wants to start a new program, rather than funding existing programs first. He wants to create a new program and our tax dollars will not go to the areas needed most, said Asa. But, Mike said that's not the case, first and foremost were going to fully fund the existing program, he said. The weekly cost of quality full day Pre-kindergarten is $140.00 according to Ross' plan.

Okay, I read the plan of both Ross and Hutchinson about Pre-K. It took me back to again living it. Our community struggles paying $40.00 a week. My mama owned a childcare center for years. Elaine's First Step on E. 16th Street in North Little Rock.

In my younger years I watched young mothers struggle to pay for childcare and it is true vouchers are much needed. Most single black parents cannot afford to place our children in the quality centers that I see in the Lakewood, Crestwood, Chenal, Shannon Hills, Cantrell, and other nice areas.

Asa argues that rather than funding existing programs, he wants to first create a new program and our tax dollars would not go to the areas with high poverty. His idea is to get the funding first and then we can expand programs. I liked Asa's comment. We need it in our community not today, but yesterday. Who's really speaking on truth? Or does this sound too good to get a vote to win?

Even though I'm not a Republican, we must compromise sometimes on what we really need in our community. I get so sick of these false articles, advertisements, and commercials to our American voters to get a win. The newspaper doesn't always state the truth. People are quick to pick up the paper and believe what most journalists have written to get a good read which causes us to begin texting, calling, twitting, and Facebook feed blasting over what's not always the truth in the newspaper. We all are guilty of it. Believing the newspaper and thinking it is the truth, but again allow me to prove facts.

My newspaper article stated;

"Nightclub Owner Guilty Of '12 Bank Robbery"

"Angela Richardson, 43 years old, found guilty, sentence to 21 years. She must serve 12 before eligible for parole. I gave Marty a toy gun. The bank bandit had a gap in their teeth."

Blah, blah, blah! What the paper didn't report is how I served an entire community. Let's backspace! A born leader, an advocate for equality, a sister, a friend, a mentor, a motivational speaker, a voice for the voiceless, a role model, a promoter, an entertainer, an entrepreneur, nonjudgmental, an employer to the unemployable. Gentle, spiritual, and helped my LGBT community.

True enough, I battled an addiction for gambling that took over my life, but we all have experienced some type of addiction. To overcome any type of addiction is important in anyone's life. The state prosecutors withheld evidence. Let's backspace! A man with a history of gun charges who was arrested in North Little Rock on 12-11-12. He already had a gun charge pending and he admitted later that he uses wigs. His former lover has a gap and mustache. A name he very well lied about not knowing in the court room. They offered him a plea deal to lie under oath and testify against me. They convicted me based only on hearsay! They had no evidence against me. Nothing at all to place me behind these bars for twenty-one unjust years! Is it justice served or hearsay?

I could've very well proved the facts and walked. I truthfully admitted my involvement of driving the car because I needed to put 12-12-12 behind me. The same as I've done my gambling addiction. GOD knows without an addiction, I'm untouchable with creativity and the love of my community. I'm not the type to threaten people or harm people as the court would have you to believe with Jo-Jo's lies. My inner spirit and visions are more of a threat with fulfilling my purpose in my *lyfe"n"tyme*.

I had to take my spirit from behind these bars and I quickly took my mind elsewhere to remain humble. I thought about Monday nights at Jazzi's Nightclub sitting around the table with Sandra, Tee, Frank and others enjoying cocktails, great fish, fries, smothered potatoes and listening to The On Call Band until Haywood decided to sing *"Adore" by Prince*. I will admit that certain songs he sings are pretty good, but this song needs to be taken off of his list. My advice to him is to go through Prince's collection and try singing *"Darling Nicki" or "Scandalous"*…LOL. I miss looking over at Swinton, the security guard as we both burst out laughing at him.

Haywood thought I disliked him over his girlfriend, Tina, but the love and closeness we shared can't be talked down just like our black history can't be talked down. Nothing ever happened between me and her and he's not the first or last that felt some type of way about me over their woman. He should appreciate her because she really does love Haywood through it all. A special shout-out to the On Call Band from Newport Prison and as far as Tina, much love to the diva express and AngieSaidThat!

Chapter 24

Daddy, Father, GOD

As I continue to read the newspaper one certain article pissed me off. The nerves of this bishop! He is probably one of Bishop Eddie Long's fans and the first one to judge when he has skeletons in his very own closet. This is why I needed to get out from behind these bars and protest for our equal rights with Randi, who is over the Carr Organization on Scott Street in Little Rock. I was not only feeling some type of way for myself, but I also thought about my LGBT community and their thoughts regarding the bishop's stand on equality. The article read;

Friday, September 26, 2014

"Arkansas Catholic Diocese Wants To Enter Same-Sex Marriage Suit"

The leader of Arkansas' Roman Catholic diocese wants the state's highest court to consider his thoughts on the voter-approved same-sex marriage ban. The bishop of Little Rock asked the Arkansas Supreme Court on Thursday to accept a friend of the court brief that argues justices should uphold Arkansas' 2004 same-sex marriage ban. A state judge tossed the ban last spring.

The court brief argues that same-sex marriage bans are valid and if acted on by the people it undermines an institution that is the bedrock of any society. It challenges the state law on same-sex marriage and Pulaski County Judge Piazza's decision to strike a state law and the voters approved constitutional amendment that reserved marriage as a right exclusively shared between a man and woman.

The ruling in May 2014, prompted several hundred same-sex marriage licenses to be issued, but was suspended by the Supreme Court on May 17, 2014 ruling it erred and the laws were unconstitutional as it would allow couples such as mother and daughter, sister and sister, or brother and brother to marry, the brief states. The law was suspended until arguments could be brought before Justice Judge Piazza. As a result the ruling demeaned the democratic process that put them into effect years ago. Clerk Larry Crane filed a brief supporting Piazza's arguments that laws against gay couples' rights to marriage are discriminatory. Cheryl Maples said she has no objections to the Diocese's involvement in the case, but thinks it's position is a bit off-topic.

My stomach dropped reading this article. It wasn't any of the bishop's business who we loved or wanted to share our *lyfe"n"tyme* with. Some of these bishops are the first to judge others and submit briefs or whatever when they very well need to write a brief about their own selves.

It is no different than the Chaplin here at Newport Prison. Quick to teach, but need to be taught! Stop! Just stop telling us not to do this and that because it is so ungodly! But, it's okay for him as the Chaplain to enjoy the flesh of the inmates. Let's just keep it real people! We, the inmates get cuffed and placed in Seg, but the Chaplin gets more grant funding and thinks it's a blessing. As the song says folks, *"It Ain't The Whiskey!"*

This reminds me of the purple hull peas that Mama had us picking to find the rotten ones in the bunch. We always had to get rid of the rotten ones to enjoy the good ones with our sweet potatoes, macaroni & cheese, meatloaf, and hot water cornbread. And later that great peach cobbler! My Mama surely knew how to put her foot in some great soul food cooking. Not only for us, but for other children as well whom she opened the door to our home to. Mama's big giving heart has truly been placed inside of me and without heart surgery. She gave to and truly cared for others. And no, I do not regret giving, giving, giving! I also appreciate what GOD has blessed us all with in order to help others.

Now I see things totally different. GOD has allowed me to handle things on a different level. I no longer want to be associated with certain people who are negative and not on my level. GOD will fruitfully bless me. I don't think I'm better than anyone walking down Asher Avenue holding signs and asking for money to eat, or those living in cars wrapped up in blankets to stay warm, or at the hotel smoking crack, or at the gambling houses around town shooting dice, or drug dealers. GOD loves us all the same and I do too! I just want to be who I am without a gambling addiction, a child of GOD with a purpose in life and closer to my Creator in Jesus name.

That's all I'm going to do now that I have finally found my purpose in life after receiving a text message from my dear friend, Vona Cox. Nothing in this United States of America can stop me from fulfilling my purpose. I don't belong to the state. I am a child of GOD. *The Maury Show* has not yet revealed the spiritual father to all these women who are repeatedly looking for their baby's daddy, but I have found mine! GOD the Almighty, you are my father! AngieSaidThat

All I can think about is the scene in the movie *"The Color Purple"* where Sophia told Harpo to get back and I got this before she slapped the hell out of the mayor's wife about her nigger children. First of all, I walked over to Stephanie and asked her to tell me what the word diocese meant. I searched for it in the commissary dictionary, but there was not a definition. She said it meant like one of the highest priest. No wonder Cheryl's statement made so much sense and why did this highly priest belittle us as gays about our *lyfe"n"tyme*? This is why I will continue, even as a prisoner, to tell my LGBT community to stand for something or they will fall for anything. I'm currently in prison and surely if I'm still fighting for our rights facing twenty-one years, surely you people should be able to attend the rallies and stand with Randi.

Hey people, put your blunts down, put your Patron down, put your vodka down, put your cocaine and pills down! Go out and fight for what should be rightfully granted to us. Justice and equality in the state of Arkansas! We matter people! Stop complaining. Get off Facebook talking about your marriage until it's legal *now & later*. We must stop being afraid of what we as a whole can help change. I can't do it by myself. For the priest to say we might as well marry our very own relatives is a low blow to us as gay people. I am grateful for those who stood outside the court house with me and joined me in the month of May to watch hundreds of same-sex couples join together in matrimony on that day and experience what we all have been waiting for and wanting in our *lyfe"n"tyme*. Equality!

If these lawmakers would only allow GOD to judge us for loving someone who they think is so wrong. And even if it is wrong, I love my mate and GOD knows my heart. I don't believe he will send me to hell over it. And who is this high ranking priest to judge us?   Let's talk about the bishops for a minute. Don't tell us we can't have a bowl of fruity pebbles when you enjoy the splash or squirt of your milk product over the female parts too! We're all capable of doing the same things to get it wet. We all like the taste of the fruity pebbles, huh Barney? Therefore, I respectfully submit my brief from Newport Prison. *"Brokeback Mountain"* Bishop! Ugh! AngieSaidThat

"Chow Time!" Officer Catfish called smiling and looking like my brother, Eric. Even his ears stuck out like Eric's. The menu consisted of the famous beef, spinach, beans, rolls and apple cobbler. I quickly ate my apple cobbler and removed myself out of the chow hall. I could hear the new comers saying, "That's her, Angie, the gay club owner from Little Rock." I made up my mind to stay away from anybody or anything that could cause me to be written up.

3:00 AM

Staying awake talking to Stephanie about *lyfe"n"tyme* caused me to sleep through breakfast in which the inmates were excited about another serving of pancakes. The pancakes reminded me of a huge piece of hot water cornbread. I couldn't wait to go last week thinking about IHOP's beautiful, great tasting pancakes with butter and dripping hot syrup. Well, the bird thought he pissed, but he shitted.

Two huge pancakes with no flavor and a tablespoon full of syrup on the side, and no butter. I tore off a small piece and quickly gave mine away to another inmate and that was my last time doing that because it's a major write up to pass food. It is called traffic and trade. Chow hall indictment of pancakes! Pray for us and let's stop the judgment people in our *lyfe"n"tyme*!

Chapter 25

I Once Was Blind, But Now I See!

Sunday, I got up and hit my knees to praise him. I looked over at the narrow window with only two mounted bars to see the sunlight. I haven't been outside since I got moved. I have no clue as to what the weather feels like right now. I folded my *"O"* magazine to the page with her covered in red fabric and laid on my bed. Oprah had no clue that a lesbian was lying in bed with her in Newport Prison. Missy tried taking my magazine saying, "I'm getting rid of her now, Angie." Keisha held it high in the air so that Missy couldn't reach it. I wouldn't allow the other inmates to read my *"O"* magazine. I didn't want any wrinkles or torn pages. I watched some inmates cut out of magazines to create book markers with crafty words and other creations. I kept my *"O"* magazine next to me at all times as well as my wife's lips that she kissed and placed on a piece of paper and e-mailed to me. The thought of not being able to visit with my wife really had me feeling some type of way, but I couldn't stop writing to enlighten my community and fulfill my purpose and my promise to GOD in Jesus name.

To receive a letter from my friend, Gaye Sanders, made my heart truly thankful for her. She too had become a part of the AngieSaidThat movement. I'm truly the black gay community activist and you would think that mail would be overflowing from my people as well as the courtroom overflowing with people from the LGBT community during my two day trail, but GOD allowed me to see what I couldn't see before. I once was blind, but know I see.

GOD knows my heart and he spiritually created something in me which I had no clue about all of these years. My blessed gift and special talent for writing! My purpose in *lyfe"n"tyme*. He used someone I've always admired since I was eighteen years old and to this day her opinions and words have such an effect on my *lyfe"n"tyme*.

Her text had me, even as a prisoner, searching for my purpose in lyfe in Newport Prison.

Chapter 26

Underage Consent

I've stayed up day and night writing books, but not about the facts of the election time. By the time my books are released we will have new lawmakers, a new governor and possibly a new president. It's only so much I can do behind these bars, but I'm determined to get them typed, edited, and published. GOD will make sure my 12-12-12 series of books are placed in the right hands and read by many. I didn't come to Newport Prison to find a lover or get caught in the middle of the drama in this prison. GOD ain't done with me yet!

After talking to Stephanie until the early AM hours and later listening to Sir Charles' song, *"Better or Worse"*, our conversation played in my mind.

"What happened in your marriage after twenty years? Y'all were high school sweethearts, how did it go wrong?" I asked.

"Well, his career. He worked a lot. He was a supervisor on his job at the postal service. This caused him to travel one hour to work and one hour back from Conway to Cabot. My studies plus being a fulltime mother took up so much of my much time and we barely saw one another. He didn't have time to attend any of our children's sports, school activities, or anything. It was all about his career. I mean he became very negative about sports with our kids and their goals were not important. We started to argue all the time. We tried to make

Wednesdays our evening out together for dinner, but that didn't work out. So we decided to give each other time away. I moved into my grandmother's home. Nobody lived there and it's still empty now. We needed time from one another. He wouldn't even take care of our little weenie dog while I took the children to their games or while me and the kids were traveling. So this is how I started with Jay, the seventeen year-old. He always complained about how his parents made him get a job. He felt like they made him a man too soon with a lot of responsibilities. So later on it just happened." She explained.

"Stephanie, how did the school and your husband find out? I asked.

"It was a Tuesday night. I got a phone call from my principal at the central administrative office. He told me that I needed to come and talk to him. He never said why. I asked him if I needed to get a student's file together and he said no. I agreed to come, but I couldn't understand why he didn't tell me what it was about. I texted Jay, but he didn't reply back. I called him. No answer. One of my friends, a resource teacher, showed up at my house and told me about the allegations that were being made. I asked her if they were going to press charges and she said not as of yet."

"So, what about your husband?" I asked.

"Well, I went over to our house and told him all about it. He called me selfish and told me I didn't think about our kids. I only thought about myself. He told me to pack the rest of my shit and get out." She explained.

"Why didn't you just get probation? I find myself looking at you because I've listened to you talk and you seem so squeaky clean. You are intelligent. You are someone with two master's degrees and a bachelor's degree. Your family is so supportive and you have three beautiful children. Tell me how do you feel about this SOFT program that you have to attend or there is a chance you will be stipulated to be here another year and even denied on your parole hearing?" I asked.

"I'm angry about it, to have to be in there with those women and I don't understand why. Angie, one woman used a dildo on her three year old baby girl." She replied.

"Wait a minute! Is she tall, blonde hair, and weird eyes? I asked.

"Yes." She answered.

"I was in Barrack 2 with her. I tried to use the restroom one morning while she was on clean up. I couldn't stop looking at the broom in her hand. I watched her screw the mop together and I became constipated." I explained to Stephanie.

"I asked her in the class why she did that and what was she thinking. She told us that she really wanted to get revenge on her ex-husband and during the times their daughter went over to visit him she would act out so badly that he couldn't control her. She's attracted to children. She admitted that even while watching Disney movies get her worked up." She stated.

"Stephanie, are you kidding me? You telling me this and that woman wanted to play in my hair in Barrack 2. She is a sick woman! See, that's a mess!" I stated.

"Well, Angie, there is another woman who sold her nine year old daughter's body for $20.00 worth of meth." She stated.

I said to her, "Stephanie, I don't think what you did is wrong. After all he was a sexually active seventeen year old young man. He's now twenty-one years old and might have a sixteen year old pregnant right now. Why isn't he in prison and how does his parents feel about that? Stephanie, to be honest I don't think that you belong in that program or in this prison. The fact is, this young man was already sexually active and you didn't have to guide him on where to put his penis or on what makes a female body go boom, boom, boom! Unlike a three year old child!"

These are issues that our lawmakers should be concerned about at election time versus funding for Pre-K that cost $140.00 per week.

We can always upgrade and reconstruct property, but not our children's body parts, mind, soul, or their cries. I'm so sick of the newspaper and commercials telling the American voters lies. I assume Stephanie's people didn't have connections or wasn't childhood friends of any of our elected politicians. They are quick to use the media in which the nature of the American press has quickly changed over the years with all of this modern technology.

First, it was the telegraph, then telephones, then computers and satellites. And to think of the idea of journalism as a profession when many journalists have no clue or facts as to what the truth really is, only their opinions. It is *tyme "n" lyfe* to keep it real with our American people. Just as telephones and computers have changed our world, what about our community needs and our troubled youth needs? If the politicians say to our American people during election that our insurance, education, and childcare programs will decrease by 20%, please don't give us 15% or 25%. Give us the 20% as promised. Stop trying to get a vote off what most voters want to hear. Just keep it real!

"Stephanie, with your credentials, educational background from ASU, and experience in the school districts, tell me how you feel about sex education in our schools? You know most parents want to think it is not their child at 12 years or younger having sex, but the reality is, yes it is your child." I asked.

"It needs to be taught to our children. Even me knowing at the age of fifteen that my daughter had sex, I didn't want to believe it. I mean the boy was sixteen, but we as parents don't want to believe that our children are sexually active." She stated.

In the state of Arkansas, Christian beliefs and education wins our lawmaker's hearts and most of them will not dare admit that their child has an addiction, is gay, or sexually active to our American voters. Let's find ways to target and help what's happening today, tomorrow, *now & later*. In reality, we must help our youth. We need to develop new programs for these issues.

I'm sure if a black seventeen year old was having sex with his teacher, most likely and trust me, if the daddy is around he's thinking, *"That's my boy, you took after your daddy, and I hope you get good grades in her class!"*

On the other hand, Stephanie's prosecutor, a white man told her attorney. "I don't want her to go to prison, but how can I go and face my church members."

"Wow! What did your case have to do with his church or the price of tea in China? I asked.

"Well, this is how some people think and he's a member of one the largest Baptist churches." She stated.

"I know why you're angry, but you have to get back in that program if that's what you need to go home. It's all about the paperwork, just like the Friday morning safety meetings. The signature is what's important. That's why so many grant funding programs are being misused and the American taxpayer's money. We need to talk about the truth around election time." I said.

"Stephanie, I dropped to my knees and prayed for you last night. We are all capable of making mistakes, but this was consensual sex. You shouldn't have to register as a sex offender nor should your career be over at the age of thirty-nine. You rightfully studied and earned your educational degrees. We all fall short and I would love to have you around my nieces and nephews, unlike those women with the Walt Disney fantasies and sticking dildos in her child. They must not know that Mickey Mouse and Donald Duck will beat their sick asses over the children. They are both sick! Stephanie, keep your spirit prayed up. I can't blame the young man for wanting to enjoy other studies besides his books, the female parts of the skeleton's scientific movements of the pelvic bones." I said and we both laughed.

"Angie, I wish you could talk to my judge." She said laughing.

"Maybe he will read my book." I replied also laughing. "So, do you think you and your ex-husband can remain friends at this point?" I asked.

"No! He had me crying over the phone the first few weeks of being here. He's negative towards me and I care not to hear from him. A week after I got here he mailed me my divorce papers. I have someone I love now, I found someone to give me something he never could emotionally, and that is just to listen to me. I love Amberly. My family and my children accept her. We will be together outside of this prison." She stated.

"Sometimes leaving is easy. As long as we get to say goodbye, I really don't care. Say I'm a liar, a cheater, anything you want." Lyrics of truth by Chrisette Michelle in this *lyfe"n"tyme*.

Chapter 27

GOD Is My Judge

Sunday Night

Tonight Monique was lying in bunk 37 and she had the largest tits I've seen yet. She took out her right breast and started sucking it. She also started playing with her nipples and bouncing her titties around.

I yelled out. "Throw dem tits in a circle!" We all laughed, but what I didn't know was that Missy, Stephanie, and all the women except for five in Barrack 13 wanted me to perform a striptease in my state provided thermals.

Well, with my creative expertise, I put on Sta-Day's knee-high rubber knee-high kitchen boots, my thermal pants, and my sports bra. I tuned the MP4 player to *"Slow"* by Jamie Foxx and placed the sock down my pants that Dale kept her pads in. She formed them into the different objects of her choice. I thought of two of my favorite stud strippers, Pretty P. and Cashmere, and their seductive moves played in my mind. I allowed my body to move like a snake listening to Jamie Foxx lyrics, *"I'm a take it slow, let you get yours then I will get mine."*

I can honestly say the inmates truly enjoyed watching me. I placed one white girl on her back and danced between her legs. She couldn't keep her eyes off me as I grabbed her closer! I also grabbed,

Dale, a plus size black female who has a hearing and speech disability and performed a lap dance for her.

She looked up at me and said trying to get her words out in slow motion. "I'm, I'm, I'm, I'm on my period and you just messed my pad up, Angie! It's done moved to the back!" We all cried laughing.

Some of the women that I entertained have been locked up anywhere from two to ten years. I took a chance of getting written up, but what is wrong with a little laughter and entertainment behind these white walls?

My freedom is already taken, but the system cannot take away my sense of humor, my creativity, my gifted comedian talent, or my gift of writing. GOD created this spirit in me and formed it into what all races, colors, and genders love about me. I'm different which has caused other studs to dislike me. They dislike me for being me, even here in prison! But it's okay, I'm Moxie! I have the ability to face problems with the best of spirits.

I have helped the informant in my case out of love and the goodness of my heart, the same way I have done for most. I have heard that he has colored his hair blonde now, but the blonde hair still doesn't make his hating and lying ass AngieSaidThat! The same goes for another one of Little Rock's stud, KO Dior, whom I allowed to join my promotion team again after she burned me once before. I truly forgave her the first time. Yes, many things that we do disturb GOD and Jesus both, but they are both so forgiving of us. Even now that I'm passed this court mess, there are those who still envy me for being someone that no one can control but GOD. GOD created me and made me gifted and talented for a purpose!

We all have allowed Satan to interfere with our spirit in the midst of finding our purpose in *lyfe "n" tyme*. I was once a team player for

Satan. We all are human, but at some point if your life isn't making sense, it's time to let go and let GOD!

The AngieSaidThat movement didn't come to an end as many have Facebooked, gossiped, tweeted, texted, and called talking about. What people fail to realize is that I could care less what anyone has to say. GOD is my judge. At this time he could've chosen anyone to do this job behind these bars, even a staff member, but He knew who would be focused on their mission of letting the readers, lawmakers, voters, criminals, media, church folks, and overall the people know what's going on behind these bars and in our politics. I am protected by GOD as David protected his sheep and I fear no evil.

No one promised me that the journey of my *lyfe"n"tyme* would be easy. He knows our weakness, but my Bible teaches me that when GOD steps into our lives and we truly have faith in Him, that all things are possible.

I cannot lie and say that tears haven't fallen from my eyes during this situation, even on June 4, 2014, although the prosecutor stated that I, Angela Richardson, showed no remorse. I'm not by far angry at anyone in that courtroom. The fact is, none of them knew me and no, I didn't show any remorse sitting there listening to all the lies, but not hearing or seeing any of the evidence that was hidden from the jurors. Plus, the rumor has it in our community, that this same judge on my case has worn an ankle monitor, been accused of drinking, using cocaine, and dealing with prostitution issues of his own. He is truly talked about in our community. Is he angry over the fact that he really hates his own issues? We all are human regardless if we are getting paid or not. It's called *lyfe"n"tyme*.

We are all on borrowed time and honestly all I'm asking him and others that hold these positions to do is just be fair with their positions of authority when they hand out justice. Nothing more, nothing less! I'm not in need of a favor from anyone at this point in my life. GOD has shown me favor, even in prison in Newport, Arkansas.

After a visit my attorney friend Stanley made the comment. "You will go to Newport and run that place." He stated this as he smiled and walked out of the county jail at 3201 W. Roosevelt. I didn't plan on running this prison. There are far too many unfair issues in this place, plus, these rules and programs are so outdated.

I fully understand Stephanie's reasons for disliking the SOFT program due to her educational background and her career in education. Unlike our Chaplin and other staff members who started off as security officers. We all can read the Bible and get people to listen, but was it the love of GOD that had him coming to deliver his words? Or was it the lust for these female prisoners and plenty of grant money that had the Chaplin saying Amen in Jesus name after the great taste of the commissary female prisoner's flesh or the hot taste of inmate counsel female peppers? You hypocrite!

Chapter 28

It's A Family Affair

The employee over the sex offender program used to work in classification. My point is that I understand how people move up on their jobs if there are certain positions opened to apply for and you meet the qualifications of X, Y, and Z.

For example; you work at McDonald's on the fries and burgers. You're never late, a great worker and three months later you're working up front on the register. Your work skills prove you're great with customers and your customer service skills are priceless. In four months you're a team lead and able to train others, plus you love your job. Within a year you are an assistant manager with another $.50 cent raise. You have a new uniform with a bowtie and the arch and the "M" pinned to your collar. The customers and employees love your smile and the regular customers look forward to seeing you during breakfast as they enjoy a great sausage McMuffin, hash brown, a cup of coffee, and a good cinnamon roll.

"So, would you like to supersize that order, Sir? Thank you and enjoy your breakfast." You say with a smile and great customer service.

A year later you're the store manager. Two years later you're the general manager. To move up like that is great! However, does it ever cross your mind with being so good at building someone else's vision and dreams, to later take that experience and build your own?

But, it's all family related in this prison. These people have these positions without having the proper education or experience, but we as inmates have to respect and understand their positions. The most qualified applicant should have a better chance on the bids of most positions, but sometimes it's not all about what you know, but who you know. That's why I no longer try to get the warden's, the captain's, the major, or anyone else's attention anymore. All I need is the public's attention for my vision of writing a series of books to become reality in a matter of time. It's time to try GOD, *now & later!* AngieSaidThat

Chapter 29

"It Ain't the Whiskey"

It's about our American taxpayer's dollars and the troubled youth with me. It's truly about the fakeness of our candidates, the untrue newspaper articles, and false media coverage. So, if the State of Arkansas want to get on the map, let's travel the world with AngieSaidThat and give me my fair share of justice. And GOD knows twenty-one years isn't anywhere near justice in my case. I've proven nothing but facts. I've studied my basic concepts. Elections serve three major purposes in an organization or political system.

First and most obviously, they provide a mechanism for selecting leaders and for helping to set the broad course of public policy. Whether the elections are the best method for making such decisions is an open question. It depends on the nature of the decision, the commitment of the electorate, and the availability of alternate mechanisms. Elections are used as a way for voters to pass legislation directly or ratify decisions made by their elected representatives.

Secondly, election provides a key check on public officials. Merely knowing that an election will be held may profoundly affect the behavior of political leaders. More commonly, the need for constant re-election might lead the official to court voters actively and constantly. Asking successful politicians why they read about re-election is like asking the rich why they clip coupons. That's how they got where they are in the first place. Knowing my sister LaShay needed those coupons with a household of three.

Finally, elections serve to legitimize the exercise of political power. Citizens who have a say in the government process may be more likely to accept the regime as lawful and most likely to obey its rules and regulations. Having the chance to participate in political decision making may strengthen the bond between the citizen and the government. And it may create stronger feelings of community among those participating.

This is why I need to be back in our community. We all need to know the truth. Not what most are reading, watching, and voting on that later becomes a joke to most of our people. However, to keep it real with my readers, I state the facts. *"It Ain't The Whiskey!"*

Chapter 30

Be Careful Of Your Surroundings

Monday, September 29, 2014

"Chow Time!" The office yelled.

I didn't even open my eyes and I covered my head. I quickly took out time last night to fold my blanket so I wouldn't be worried about oversleeping as far as my bed being in order. Beds must be in order by 7 AM on weekdays and 9 AM on weekends. We stay covered up in this cold prison in our state issued jackets and robes trying to remain warm. A few have been written up and placed on restrictions for being two minutes late lying under their blankets.

Finally awake, I prayed and got up to brush my teeth and wash my face. Others were out in the field, at school, or whatever. I had a dentist appointment at 3:45 PM scheduled on the daily layout sheet. Last night I took one of Missy's pills. A small yellow and white capsule with a Tylenol pretending I was high too. This is a prime example of trying to fit in so others will think you're so cool, even in prison.

We sipped tea and Kool-Aid as if it was a good Tom Collins. It's important to watch your surroundings, folks. I'm speaking to all my youth, even if it's fun at the time. What if I enjoyed the feeling of the unknown pills? There is no telling what I would do in this prison to get my own. Not to mention they do drug testing in prison, the same as most employers do. But, it's not worth the outcome of going to the hole, being placed on restrictions, or not having the daily job over making bad decisions.

Sometimes the person who wants you to get that good feeling too may cause you harm and Missy gets her way around here. I picked up and read one of Missy's many major disciplinary write-ups. It read;

Self-mutilation, creating unnecessary noise, possession/introduction of staff uniforms or clothing resembling staff uniforms, or unauthorized civilian clothing or identification. And deliberately giving misinformation or falsely accusing another in the course of an official investigation.

Incident Report

June 12, 2014   10:00 PM   McPherson Unit

On 06/12/14 at approximately 10:00 PM, I Sgt. Meeks, was working Zone Four- Segregation. I went to Cell 243 assigned to Inmate Missy Rock. She had a blanket covering her hand and her upper body and refused to take the blanket off. I then radio for responders. Nurse Mole and Nurse Low arrived with a stretcher. When security arrived, Lt. Chapstick called for Cell 243 to be opened. When security entered the cell Inmate Missy Rock removed what appeared to be a torn up sheet from her neck. She was placed in handcuffs and secured in the showers. Hand restraints were then removed and Inmate Rock was evaluated by medical staff.

While secured in the showers, Inmate Rock and Inmate Turner, who was secured in the top shower, were yelling to each other and Turner told Rock not to talk to security or tell them anything. They were also discussing what cells they were going to be placed in as their intent to manipulate staff into a housing move. Inmate Missy Rock on behavior control status persuaded the major and she was returned to Cell 243 after all property was removed and the cell had been searched. Therefore Sgt. Meeks charged Missy Rock with all charges listed above.

Even after serving time in the pits of this prison, Missy to this day is the favorite of many as long as she's not involved with the black studs. We all know in front of the media it would be a different story. I'm here living it and have always been around it, but who am I in the eyes of those with authority and our American voters? GOD see things so differently. Even the high ranking priest with his brief stands against same-sex marriages. I am a child of God and will be getting married regardless to my female lover, Valerie! In Jesus name. Amen.

So if you are such a man of GOD stop judging us and come marry us in your priest black and white attire, Bishop! Bring your anointing oil to bless us with bountiful blessings and AngieSaidThat!

Chapter 31

What Size Do You Wear?

Readers, please follow me with proven facts and as I tell you that July 16, 2014, was most definitely life-changing for me as I entered the gates of the Newport Prison Compound.

"What size bra, shoes, pants, and shirt do you wear?" She asked with a clipboard in her hand.

LeLe Robertson is thirty-nine years old and has served sixteen years with five more to do under the 70% law.

Why hasn't it changed in the State of Arkansas? Is Beebe against it too? Well, his time is up and we pray from the heart and mercy of our fight that our newly elected governor of the state of Arkansas listens to *"The Cries behind the Bars"*.

Lele, who had no clue of the meaning of *lyfe"n"tyme* back then, is an innocent person who was unable to read and write, but learned how to count from a prison flower bed.

Chapter 32

LeLe's Sisterly Love

September 27, 2014, 7:05 PM was tuned into listening to CeCe Winans' song, *"Alabaster Box"* and reading the following documentation.

In the Circuit Court of Phillips County Arkansas   The State vs LeLe Robertson

Motion of suppressed statement of the defendant comes. The defendant LeLe Robertson is charged with capital murder and aggravated robbery. The defendant was arrested on June 17, 1997. Subsequently, the arresting members of the County Sheriff's Office and the Arkansas State police conducted custodial interrogations of the defendant. Counsel for her defense anticipates the statement made during these interrogations will be offered into evidence against the defendant at the trial of this matter.

Statements should be suppressed for the following reasons: The police did not have probable cause to arrest or detain the defendant. Rule 7.1 requires among other things that from the affidavit there be reasonable cause to believe an offense has been committed. Any statements which are the fruits of such illegal arrest are inadmissible against the defendant. The defendant was not properly advised of her constitutional rights in accordance with the Miranda Law. And if said rights were given the defendant did not knowingly, intelligently, or voluntarily waive said constitutional rights. The statements were the result of coercion meeting (force), physical intimidation, physical force, and unauthorized promises of leniency by members of the Phillips County Sheriff's Office and Arkansas State Police making statements that were involuntary and inadmissible for any purpose.

The defendant was denied her 6th and 14th Amendment rights to counsel during phases of interrogation making said statements inadmissible.

Wherefore, the defendant prays that for the above reasons her motion to suppress the statement of defendant be granted.

Respectfully Submitted, February 17, 1999

Readers, please follow me with this story. The following are statements from LeLe's youngest sister, Lynn. This statement was taken in June 1997 at 5:05 PM at the Helena Police Department. Present were Captain Devon and Larry Smith, Assistant Chief of Police.

Q.   *State your name.*

A.   *Lynn Brown.*

Q.   *Lynn, what is your address?*

A.   *I don't know.*

Q.   *Where do you live?*

A.   *On Cherry Street.*

Q.   *What is your date of birth?*

A.   *February 16, 1981.*

Q.   *February 16, 1981?*

A.   *Uh huh.*

Q.   *Lynn, you understand that I'm intending to ask you some questions about a murder that occurred on March 30, 1997?*

A.   *Yes, sir.*

Q.   *Off Essie Street?*

A.   *Yes, sir.*

Q.   *Have you been read your rights?*

A.   *Yes, sir.*

Q.   *Do you understand your rights?*

A.   *Yes, sir.*

Q.   *Is there anything about your rights that you want explained to you?*

A.   *No, sir.*

Q.   *Are you aware that this statement is being recorded?*

A.   *Huh?*

Q.   *Do you know that we are recording this?*

A.   *Yes, sir.*

Q.   *Okay, is that alright with you?*

A.   *Yes, sir.*

Q.   *Lynn, tell me what you know about the murder that occurred.*

A.   *Well, me and Chris and Tonya we had walked over Willie's house and Chris went in the kitchen to get a knife. Then Willie had asked Chris what she was doing with his knife. And she said that she was going to do something with it. So she came around there and got us and we had walked over the levee when we seen that girl name Essence. Me and Chris had walked up there and asked if she was still talking to Sleepy. And then Chris cut the girl. We didn't hold her down or nothing. That's all me and Tonya did was got her money out of her pocket.*

Q.   *When you're talking about Chris. What's Chris last name?*

A.   *Robertson.*

Q.   *When you're talking about Tonya, what's her last name?*

A.   *Robertson.*

Q.   *Tonya Robertson?*

A.   *Uh huh.*

Q. Alright. What time did you all see Essence?

A. Downtown.

Q. About what time was that?

A. 12 or 1 in the morning.

Q. 12 or 1 in the morning?

A. Uh huh. It was around 1.

Q. Alright. Where downtown did you see her?

A. Down there by Larry's.

Q. Larry's Liquor Store.

A. Uh huh.

Q. Alright, then you saw her again?

A. Yes, sir.

Q. Where did you see her?

A. Across the levee.

Q. Tell me what happened across the levee.

A. Her and Chris got to arguing. They got to fighting. Chris had caught her and grabbed her by her hair and throwed her on the ground.

Q. Essence and Chris?

A. Yeah, Essence and Chris. Then Essence ran behind the house and then Chris did.

Q. Is this the house over on Ohio Street that you're talking about?

A. Yes, sir. And I believe that she got stabbed in the arm somewhere. It was somewhere. I know that.

Q. You saw Chris stab her?

144

A.   Yes, sir.

Q.   All of it took place behind the house?

A.   No, in the front. It began at the front then Essence ran to the back. Then
        Chris caught her and grabbed her by her hair and pulled her down.
Q.   Where were you and Tonya at this time?

A.   We was just coming to the back. We was walking. At first we was in the front.
        Then they ran. Then me and Tonya we walked around there.
        After we seen that she was bleeding and blood was on the knife. So I had asked
        Chris was some money in her pocket. She said she didn't know. So me and
        Tonya went back there and checked her and it was some money in her pocket.
        A hundred dollar bill.

Q.   You and Tonya and Chris saw Essence on Ohio Street in front of the house?

A.   Yes, sir.

Q.   Alright. They got to arguing in front of the house and fighting?

A.   Yes, sir.

Q.   What were they fighting about?

A.   Over Sleepy.

Q.   Fighting about Chris' boyfriend?

A.   Yes, sir.

Q.   Then you saw Chris stab her?

A.   Yes, sir.

Q.   That was in front of the house?

A.   It was in the back of the house.

Q.   They started fighting in the front?

A.   Uh huh.

Q.   And Essence ran to the back?

A.   *Yeah.*

Q.   *Alright. Where did you see Chris stab her?*

A.   *I believe she got stabbed in the arm somewhere.*

Q.   *Anywhere else?*

A.   *I couldn't tell. She got stabbed somewhere.*

Q.   *You said you saw blood on the knife?*

A.   *Yes, sir.*

Q.   *Do you know where the knife is now?*

A.   *No, sir.*

Q.   When uh, you and Tonya were getting the money out of her pocket, out of Essence pocket, where was she at then?

A.   *On the ground.*

Q.   *In front of the house or behind the house?*

A.   *On the back.*

Q.   *Was she bleeding?*

A.   *Yes, sir.*

Q.   *Was she conscious or unconscious?*

A.   *She wasn't saying nothing.*

Q.   *She was laying there on the ground?*

A.   *Yes, sir.*

Q.   Alright. What was Chris doing while you and Tonya were getting the money?

A.   *She was waiting for us. Then she ran off somewhere.*

Q.   *She ran off?*

A.   *Yes, sir.*

Q.   *And what did you all do with the money?*

A.   *Spent it.*

Q.   *Spent it?*

A.   *Yes, sir.*

Q.   *Did you all split it up between you?*

A.   *Yes, sir.*

Q.   *All three of you?*

A.   *Yes, sir.*

Q.   *Did you see anybody hit her with anything? A stick, brick, or anything like that?*

A.   *No, sir.*

Q.   *When you all left the scene of where Essence was at, do you know if she was alive or not at that time?*

A.   *No, sir.   I do not know.*

Q.   *You don't know?*

A.   *No, sir.*

Q.   *Okay. Is there anything that you want to add to this statement?*

A.   *No, sir.*

Q.   *Is there anything that you haven't told me that you might want to tell me?*

A.   *No. That's all.*

Q.   *That's all?*

A.   *Yes, sir.*

Q.   *Did you ever hit or stab or do anything to Essence?*

A.   \ *No.*

Q.   *Did Tonya?*

A.   *Nope.*

Q.   *Just...*

A.   *Chris.*

Q.   *Chris did?*

A.   *Uh huh.*

Q.   *And you all took her money?*

A.   *Yes, sir.*

Q.   *What relation are you to Chris?*

A.   *My sister.*

Q.   *Are you related to Tonya?*

A.   *My sister.*

Q.   *All three of you are sisters?*

A.   *Yes, sir.*

Q.   *Do you all live in the same house?*

A.   *No, sir. Me and Tonya do.*

Q.   *Alright. And where does Chris live?*

A.   *She stay across the levee somewhere.*

Q.   *Anything else you want to add to this statement?*

A.   *No, Sir.*

Q.   *Any questions you want to ask Captain Devon?*

A.   *No.*

Q.   *Okay. You made the statements on your own free will?*

A.   *Yes, sir.*

This is the end of the statement and LeLe Robertson's name was never mentioned in the interview. This is a family of eleven with no father around. Chris is the oldest of Lynn and Tonya. She's also nine years older than LeLe.

LeLe came home to visit and found out that her two baby sisters were in jail for murder. She went to visit her sisters in jail and promised them both that she would take their charges. Chris, the oldest of the three, was smart enough not to admit her involvement in the fight with Essence for sleeping with Sleepy, her boyfriend and baby's daddy.

LeLe at the age of nearly nineteen was unable to read or write. She repeatedly told the judge and prosecutor that she did it all, even taking the money. The three sisters were convicted of aggravated robbery and murder. All three at one point were together at Newport Prison.

Due to the fact of LeLe admitting that she killed Essence, she got the most time. She has to serve twenty-one years before being eligible for parole. While serving time Lynn, who was able to read and write, taught LeLe how to count doing their hour of activity time by counting flowers, leaves, and the taste of the bitterness and sweetness of grass. She explained that it was rabbit food to prepare her to get her GED. She later would meet her in the library to teach her to read. She would make her get harder and harder books. Her instructor explained to her in math how to separate the furniture and to add a piece or take a piece away until it added up into a nice sectional. It took LeLe thirteen years to accomplish her goal of getting what she wanted more than *lyfe"n"tyme* itself, to learn how to read and write! She received her GED and is currently on the waiting list to take Vo-Tech college classes.

LeLe was innocent, but plead guilty for the protection of and out of sisterly love for her two younger sisters.

Chapter 33

Forgiveness

LeLe came home to visit for Christmas, but the Santa Clause wasn't what she expected! Her sisters, Tonya and Lynn, both served less than eight years and she hasn't heard from either of them yet. She told me far as she knows they live together until this day.

As far as Chris, the oldest of the three, she later served less than two years on other charges that had nothing to do with the case that caused her three younger sisters *lyfe"n"tyme*. She finally asked LeLe to forgive her and all four of the sisters walked behind this yellow line in all white without commissary. LeLe told her the only way she would forgive her was if she apologized to the younger sisters, which she did.

Lele wholeheartedly has forgiven her older sister. She has at least three different jobs without pay or even commissary, but even if she's sick with a cold, she gets up early in the morning and goes to her prison jobs faithfully.

Her personality is priceless. She smiles proudly with big buck teeth which are unforgettable and a heart as big as the sea.

My spirit connected with her from the day she held the clipboard up asking what size? She has no idea that she has caused me many tears. To look at her playful and spiritual ways and knowing the fact nobody in her family even writes. Her mother has nothing to do with her because she was in resource classes in the past. But she is now reading the books of her choice. Every night she now helps others with algebra. She is no longer a resource child. Who can we call on besides GOD to hear the cries behind bars?

LeLe would make anyone a great and loyal employee, but who wants to hire someone that the system has put the horrible reputation of a killer behind their name. You have read facts. She never killed anyone or robbed anyone in her *lyfe"n"tyme*.

People, please bless my books and I will see that LeLe also get a blessing. She is one that I have placed under my wings in this prison. She has taken a special place in my heart already. I feel for her. To think about my very own baby sister, Monique Norwood, there would be no questions asked, I would've done the same thing. And also thinking about my other younger sister, Dashunda, and how she loved her kids so much. If I had it my way, I would've taken her place to be next to my Mama again, but GOD has his way with us all, *now & later*.

Again, I picked up the newspaper and read what has fooled our American people. I was once one of those people who thought those in prison deserves their share of punishment, but I have taken this *tyme"n"lyfe* to enlighten the public of the truth. AngieSaidThat

Chapter 34

Covered & Smothered

I must say of my 12-12-12 series of books, LeLe's story is one of the hardest ones I have written, beside the story of Alex, the young lady who killed her mother with three different guns. GOD placed me behind these walls for a reason. Not for the reason that on June 4, 2014 caused me twenty-one years of unjust time. We need help!

I am feeling some type of way about so much and I need to ask my readers if they ever find themselves also feeling helpless in certain moments in time? To think how the media sometimes say you're safe by suggesting all the criminals, killers, child molesters, robbers, drug dealers, and bad people are locked up. They are not all locked away behind these bars. Some are just never caught and are still amongst you outside these walls. People are only doing what they do on a daily basis. Getting up and looking forward to another day. Never have I thought about nor have I ever hurt anyone. Never! Threatened to use a gun on someone? Never! And to pick up the newspaper today and see this beautiful woman who instantly and truly made my mind flashback to one of Little Rock's best news anchors, Ann Pressly, may she RIP.   Reading that another beautiful woman with a beautiful smile, who probably simply enjoyed selling homes, was missing sadden my heart. She was just as beautiful as Ann Pressly, with a great smile, blonde hair, and appeared happy. The article read;

Car and purse found at vacant home in Scott, Arkansas. Realtor Beverly Carter called her husband around 5:30 PM and told him that she was meeting a potential client on Old River Drive. They lived in Scott and being familiar with the area at 9:00 PM her husband started to worry. She should have been home. He drove to the address and her 2014 Cadillac SRX was parked in the driveway. The home was unlocked. He looked around but found no signs of his wife.

As I continued to read the article I dropped to my knees praying mercifully for her family and friends to have closure in finding the North Little Rock, Arkansas realtor. I prayed for a safe return, but the following day I awaken to bad news that I could feel the pain of thinking about my very own sister, Dashunda Richardson, who was killed on Valentine's Day in 2004. We sometimes question GOD's work, but the devil is around us on a daily basis. We often want to know why bad things happen to such good people. I did at one point, but now I faithfully tell the Lord.

"Yes, I've made up in my mind I'll say yes, my soul says yes, my mind says, my heart says yes, yes, yes I will Jesus." I tuned in listening to the lyrics of Shekinah Glory Ministry. My prayers are with her family even as a prisoner, *now & later.*

I know that some of us need to be out from behind these walls and there are some who get out and repeatedly commit such hideous crimes which affects us all in all white. Their actions draw attention and the system try to crack down on people who are out on parole. What happens when the authority doesn't listen? Is it right that other crimes are committed every day?

For instance like the confidential informant in my case. I informed the authorities about him impersonating as a police officer with a badge, flashing blue lights, and molesting children. But they were too busy trying to plot against me and didn't even make reports of my statements that led. However, they used his incredible word which led to my arrest. He has no credibility! Is this the law! Is this how justice is served at election time?

So much is covered and smothered and some of you people will not believe the things that I will never reveal about some of our elected politicians to the American voters. And it's not because I think that someone might kill me. I'll just be another dead Negro, but I can honestly say I died doing what I believed in. And that's standing for my equal rights and my justice. My name will forever be remembered through it all. I was once told I think that I'm the black gay Dr. Martin Luther King, Jr…LOL. No, I think I'm AngieSaidThat

We both have a dream. He's free at last and my dream has just become a series of 12-12-12 books. GOD believed in me when others thought my life was over. My *lyfe 'n 'tyme* just started in Newport, Arkansas prison in Jesus name.

Again, I would like to thank all my supportive readers for following the AngieSaidThat movement and supporting my series of 12-12-12 books from Newport Prison. Shout-out to you all!

In the midst of writing, my mind searches for many reasons why so much has been hidden from the public. No one thought a black female prisoner from Newport Prison would tell the truth of *Lyfe"N"Tyme*.

GOD wants us to learn to focus on the important things in *Lyfe"N"Tyme*. Often when our Creator allows times of trials and tribulation in our lives, I believe he wants us to sit down. Maybe we are just too busy trying to do too much and getting too wrapped up in making a living. GOD will allow storms in our lives because He wants to get our attention so that we can focus on him and find our purpose in *Lyfe"N"Tyme*.

Chapter 35

Daddy's Girl

09/30/2014   8:00 PM   Barrack 13

The daughter of one of Little Rock's most well-known high roller dope boys and lover of all women is amongst the prisoners in Barrack 13. What happens when all the dope, money, cars, traveling, diamonds, gold, women, and sex turns into HIV?

She is the most beautiful daughter of Fuller. She's 5'5", 145 lbs., light skinned, short black hair, beautiful smile, thick pink lips, brown eyes, and she reminds me of B- Level's lovely wife, Shenita or Angie McIntosh. She has the similarity of the beautiful actress, Halle Berry. She is twenty-six and is sitting here with me to help educate Little Rock, Arkansas on the importance of safe sex awareness.   Daddy's baby girl is sharing her father's story with the facts in Newport Prison.

My *lyfe"n"tyme* gifted writing mind couldn't get enough of my addiction for writing and craving for my commissary ink pen. With love for it all my fingers got the best workout. My mind's spirit wanted to enjoy the energy of it all.

We all heard the rumors about the nice looking drug dealer that drove around in the hottest Hummer in the city, besides the other one driven by another well-known hustler. We all loved going to The Papermoon Strip Club watching some of the sexiest dancers work the pole. Snow, a well-known dope boy would have an umbrella inside the VIP making it rain with cash. Rumors had it that he too also has HIV, but, this isn't about him. I'm not in front of his daughter, but I'm surely in front of another beautiful woman. She's what most call mouthwatering beautiful.

In December 1999, Fuller was diagnosed with HIV. What do most men tell these women? It doesn't feel the same with a condom on. Today women, especially a lot of younger women, think it could never happen to me. Who really want it to happen to them? Nobody! But this disease shows no favoritism. Is the drug money from a high roller dope boy worth your lyfe"n"tyme?

Approximately 9:26 PM 09/30/2014 Newport Prison Barrack 13 Housing Two *Reporting live from AngieSaidThat*

"What's your name?" I asked.

"Von Morehouse." She answered.

"So, your dad's family raised you?" I asked.

"Yes, his sister took care of me." She replied.

"Where are you all from?" I asked.

"Helena, Arkansas." She answered.

"Von, does it make you feel any type of way with me sharing this story with my readers?"

"No." She answered.

"Well, tell me about your life as a daddy's girl." I asked.

"I was very sheltered, but the older I got my daddy exposed me to a lot. Uhm, I remember the time I found out my daddy sold crack cocaine. I was twelve years old and with him and one of his girlfriends going to pick up my youngest sister. She's second to the oldest, I'm the oldest." She explained.

"What happened?" I asked.

"It was almost Christmas time and my dad had some crack. Like a big bundle and a rifle. The police pulled us over. I tapped my dad on the shoulder and held my hand out. He handed me the money and I cuffed it under my sleeve. I tapped him again and put my hand out. Even at the age of twelve I knew my dad would go to jail. I wanted my dad to put the crack in my hand, and he did with the look of defeat on his face. They placed him in the back of the police car and allowed me to call my mama. During all of this he was arguing with his girlfriend. The police asked if my mama, if she was aware that I was with him. She said yes, that's her daddy." She stated.

"Uhm, so did they find the drugs?" I asked.

"No, they didn't find nothing. My mama came and got me, my little sister, and my dad."

"Then what happened?" I asked.

"My dad's lifestyle kind of slowed down, but not really. I never cared for material things. I wanted my dad to be there and to have a bond with him. We had been living in Little Rock since I was five years old." She explained.

"Did your dad have plenty of women?" I asked.

"Yes, a lot of them!" She replied.

9:35 PM

"Pill call!" The officer yelled.

Von jumped up and went to pill call. I sat at the table after a hot shower and prayed that my friend, Kim, who I hadn't heard from in almost two weeks was in good spirits and safe. I really felt some type of way after reading the long article about the North Little Rock realtor and the mind of this man responsible for her death. Even as a prisoner behind these bars and dressed in all white my stomach was weakened with thoughts about it all. I wondered what her last words were as I do Ann Pressly, my sister DaShaunda, Tami Morrison, or David Tidwell in such heinous acts of crimes. What kind of person could be so hateful? Even the thought of LeLe's story still had me feeling some type of way as a prisoner myself.

In the shower waiting to continue my interview with Von my mind raced. Earlier today watching another beautiful black woman in *lyfe"n"tyme* in her commissary make-up painting the walls of this prison was troubling to me. She's black, beautiful shoulder length hair, 5'4", 160 lbs., and built like a brick house. She took the long paint roller brush and stroked it up and down applying the white paint repeatedly on the walls and looking sexy at the same time.

Nana, another inmate whom we call mouthwatering beautiful, is from Pine Bluff, Arkansas. She's light skinned, brown eyes, and a beautiful smile with pearly white teeth. She got involved with drugs earlier in life and took the life of two people. I'm not sure what led to that as of yet. We haven't talked about it. I much rather get the story or paperwork from the horse's mouth versus the talk and rumors from others. Most people know how to make a dollar out of fifteen cents and get change. There is nothing like a group of talking and gossiping women prisoners with nothing but time on their hands. Ugh! I enjoy giving my reader the facts and the truth.

A little while later Von returned from pill call and we continued the interview.

"Von, where did you all live in Little Rock?" I asked.

"Tanya Court." She replied.

"So, tell me about your dad." I asked.

"He's good as gold and sweet as pie. There were plenty of days that he would have me rolling. He watched CNN news all day. One day my dad came into my room and saw me crying with the paper in my hand. My first thought was people die from HIV. My daddy is going to die! He just dropped his head. My dad simply had an addiction for women." She stated.

"What did he say to you?" I inquired.

"He explained it to me that he had gone to the doctor and even to a liver specialist about his drinking, but had no clue it was HIV." She answered.

"How did you feel when it hit the media about your dad infecting many women?" I asked.

"I was devastated! I was eighteen years old and in the Pulaski County Jail at the time on a failure to appear. I called home to talk to my boyfriend and his words threw me for a loop. He said what's going on is your nasty ass daddy around here giving these hoes AIDS. I hung up in his face and called my aunt. She informed me about what was going on and said my daddy was in the process of turning himself into the police." She said.

"Von, I've been told that people think you have HIV. How does it make you feel to hear that?" I asked.

"I was angry until the facts were really revealed. I ended up in Pinnacle Point Hospital. Umm huh, I was one of the top five in the Miss Teen Arkansas Pageant. I did Fashion Rock USA. I modeled for Excel. I started writing poems to let it all out, but then I started fighting." She answered.

"Did you ever in life think that you were infected?" I asked.

"No." She answered.

"Von, our people are so uneducated here in the State of Arkansas about HIV/AIDS awareness, how do you feel all these years later?" I asked.

"It is true our people are lost on awareness. I'm still angry that people will not take out the time to understand it. They are so judgmental about it because they really don't understand." She answered.

"Maybe we can change some of the people's way of thinking." I said.

"Maybe. I have to serve three years. My dad and I still write each other and I love him the same, but I worry about him a lot." She said.

"Does he have a girlfriend now?" I asked.

"He's married to the babysitter. She has never tested positive and she loves him. She moved after all this happened and lives in Texas now." She answered.

"What kind of vehicle did he drive around getting the ladies attention?" I asked.

"He drove a yellow Hummer, a gray Ford 150 truck, and a Lexus. He had plenty of money and he is very handsome. The women loved him!" She answered.

10:27 PM   Count Time

The interview has ended at this time in Barrack 13 at Newport Prison. Lights out!

I returned to my bunk with way too much on my mind. I never wanted any of my books to end. I must say there is never a dull moment with me, especially in Newport Prison interviewing some of the inmates. Just know that with my creativity at being a great host, promoter, and comedian that my writing skills are just as good and speaks for itself. This is only the beginning of my journey in my *lyfe"n"tyme*!

I awoke giving praise to my Creator and another article in the newspaper captured my attention. A Little Rock bishop, ordained by the diocese in 2009, was removed from the list of clergy members. What I do know is that the same people who judge others will be judged by GOD's law. Ugh!

Hours later at mail call there was still no letter from Kim. I thought something surely must be wrong with her. I am thankful that Nana, the painter, told me last night to consider the fact that Kim was working and that sometimes our mail runs behind and to give her time. I prayed and prayed all last night that all was well with her.

"Count time!" The officer yelled.

Chapter 36

An Angel Watching Over Me

Mail call   October 3, 2014   6:40 PM

Finally a letter from Kim and it reads;

September 30, 2014

God loves you!   I love you!

Hey Angie Bangie!

How you doing girl? I pray all is well with you and I am constantly praying for you every day. I know it's been a minute since you have heard from me and I am sorry. I've been going through myself. But I will never stop being here for you. Believe that!   I pray to GOD every day to give me the strength to continue working three jobs so I can help you. But girl it ain't been right since I went to New York spending money I didn't really have. But I trust GOD that things will get better for me. It always has.   Angie, please keep trusting GOD that it will get better for you too!

Good news! I spoke to Brenda Johnson yesterday and she said I am approved for visitation. But she said you were on restriction until October 9. I think I should be able to come see you on October 12th. If I am correct, I will be there! I got your package with your appeal. It looks to be on point raising the facts of ineffective counsel, Fink's lying ass, withholding evidence, and conflict of interest with Pecker.

You did a very good job Angie and I am proud of you! Has it been submitted to the court yet and how long before you hear anything? Valerie told me you wanted me to give her your appeal papers. So I am going to give them to her tomorrow after work (Wednesday). I am working on the book and I promise to have it all typed and saved to a disk by October 31st as planned. I promise!

Keep your head up, Angie! Know that God loves you and I love you always!

Kim

Inside there were some positive and encouraging quotes. At the bottom of one page there was a picture of my mama that was priceless! The picture was from a heart shaped charm that I had made for my mama. It had her picture in the center of it and Kim had written the words. *"This angel watches over you. She loves you."* Her handwriting was to the left of the beautiful picture and quote. Tears instantly formed in the wells of my eyes and I had a smile on my face at the same time for one reason alone. My mama was here watching over me.

One of the beautiful quotes she sent read;

"Time can be an ally or an enemy. What it becomes depends entirely upon you, your goals, and your determination to use every available minute."

Another one read;

"Life is like a camera. Focus on what's important. Capture the good times. Develop from the negatives. And if things don't work out, take another shot."

I cannot explain the feeling I have at this moment. Only two other things could top this feeling. My appeal to be granted and my wife getting my books typed and processed by our promised dates and deadlines. I taped my mama's picture and the blessed, beautiful, powerful, and strong-minded owner of the *"O"* Magazine photo to the wall above my bed. My two favorite ladies were watching over me day and night here in Newport Prison. My spirit was so happy and I just can't understand why people are yet to believe in GOD's miracles. I dare you to believe it and receive it! It's called faith, hope, and prayer. I dare you to *Tri GOD: Now & Later* in this *lyfe "n" tyme!*

Today, I got some disturbing news. I heard that after long hours of painting the prison walls, Nana got caught taking a package of Kool-Aid from the kitchen and was sent to the hole. You would think that after the long hours of painting that she would be able to have certain items, certainly something to drink.

The inmates perform all the maintenance and duties in this prison to save money. The inmates cook, serve the food, work on the heating and air, and the plumbing, etc. You can just say we do it all and at the end of the day getting some Kool-Aid shouldn't have caused her to lose her class, her job, and be placed in the pits of this prison with restrictions. I prayed for Nana, Safari, Tyna, Mina, and several others that were currently in the hole. I prayed for myself that I would never have to find out what the pits of this prison is like. GOD has his way with us all. Lord forgive me. *It ain't the Whiskey* it's called *lyfe"n"tyme!* AngieSaidThat

October 4, 2014

Any other time in my life I would be at my club on Asher Avenue in Little Rock, Arkansas. But, due to the fact of our justice system in the great State of Arkansas, unfortunately I'm writing and book clubbing in Newport Prison. I often wondered how the Bills of Rights are passed to get the voters' attention to race down to the polls to vote on the issues in our city, state, and nation.

Most of the inmates had returned from the chow-hall and some were watching my favorite movie, *"Baby Boy"*, starring Tyrese, Taraji P. Henson, and Snoop Dogg. I picked up a book with references to understanding our Bill Of Rights.

The Bill of Rights

The Bill of Rights is the collective name for the first ten amendments to the United States Constitution. Proposed to assuage the fears of Anti-Federalist who opposed Constitutional ratification, these amendments guarantee a number of personal

freedoms, limit the government's power in judicial and other proceedings, and reserve some powers to the state and the public.

Over the years, the Supreme Court has displayed great flexibility in interpreting the Constitution. For example, the 14th Amendment guarantees equal protection of the laws. It was designed primarily to protect Americans from discrimination based on race. The court has extended the amendments reach to include discrimination based on sex as well. Similarity the court has extended the meaning of each phrase to include not only spoken words, but also symbolic speech for example, burning LGBT flag as a jester of protests. It is also found a right to privacy in the very provisions of the Bill of Rights and interprets it to include a woman's and a man's right to same-sex marriages, and a woman's right to choose a woman. Many critics charge that the court has overstepped the proper bounds of its own authority.

We love Little Rock's Judge Griffin and Judge Piazza. A judge's flexibility is essential. The Bishop that respectfully submitted his brief against same-sex marriages made the statements that if the bill passed it would allow us to marry our relatives. But, is it okay for the bishop's colleague to make sexual statement to others? So, is it that some briefs are acceptable behind the curtains in your black and white attire? Sounds to me the bishop is in need of our father's briefing. Love us as he loves you, playa! Ugh!

Most need to be careful of how we represent GOD, our creator, in any religion. GOD will expose us just like he did Eve, thinking she could hide from GOD and enjoy the forbidden fruits in the garden. After Adam introduced her to the enjoyable movements of the fruit juices it produced more spirits. GOD wants us to love others as he loves us. We all need to follow GOD's law, just as the Congress follow the Bill of Rights. The Bible teaches the hand of justice instead of violence.

My friend, Denise Howard, son need justice. My nephew, Roderick Stewart, need justice. Gayle Wood's son, Bryan, need justice in order to rest in peace after being gunned down by the Maumelle Police Department. Michael Brown and Trayvon Martin families can't buy flesh or spirits with any type of state or Federal compensation for taking their sons lives. The system is quick to bring up the criminal record of someone out on parole who wants another chance in *lyfe"n"tyme*. Does this mean all police officers in crispy blue uniforms are the same wanting to gun down our young black men?

Who wants to hear the cries of a prisoner or a criminal? The Bill of Rights causes so many arguments. People, let's talk about the facts in our community. We all have a lifetime of memories, but this is for my homies that are gone. Most can't believe that you're gone and I'm so sorry you're gone, but I got to keep moving until I get there. Just the thought of it all has me and others feeling some type of way about what some call justice. I just wanted to listen to *"Gangsta Lean"* by D.R.S. Maybe GOD will see to it that justice will be served according to the Bill of Rights in the State of Arkansas and all across America. To think of the black young man in Florida killed by a white man for playing his music too loudly makes me wonder, would it have been different if he had been listening to *"It Ain't The Whiskey"*, a country song?

Chapter 37

People, Know Yourself!

"Line up for Rec!" Sgt. Ox yelled. I looked up at the clock as it struck 5:00 PM. As much as I wanted to get up and join the others the music in my ears and my commissary ink pen had me truly in my own zone. My spirit was outside of these brick white walls as I sipped on the Sprite that I had ordered from Inmate Council. I had finished eating a bean burrito that Missy made for me. I shared half of it with Von and I also enjoyed a few Chunky Chocolate Chips Ahoy cookies. It instantly took me back to Pike Street in North Little Rock to Laronda Adams' house. I tuned in listening to Sir Charles' song *"Better or Worse"*.

My mind had me going and I could only imagine what many had to say after my hurricane verdict and the big newspaper article. It is amazing how GOD exposed my purpose in my *lyfe"n"tyme* while fighting for justice. I will have an amazing comeback from this setback. Even the critics input will be changed once the truth is proven. Some of the courtrooms overstep their proper bounds by departing too much from the constitutional text. My enemies also disagreed with my unjust verdict. I wonder what will all of the people with cell phone plans with Verizon, A&T, Sprint, Cricket, Boost Mobile, Twitter, Instagram and Facebook have to say about my 12-12-12 book series of prison reality. AngieSaidThat

I couldn't withhold expressing my true feelings. People, especially my youth, get to know yourself regardless of your situations behind the bars or in the free world. The most important thing in this *lyfe"n"tyme* is finding your purpose. There is nothing more rewarding than to know your purpose and fulfill it. All that is happening in my life right now lets me know that GOD's eyes were watching me. He healed my gambling addiction and redeemed me. I could very well be sitting here in Newport Prison watching *"Baby Boy"* or asleep knowing that justice has not been equally or fairly served to me. There are plenty of inmates that need my voice to be heard publicly on their behalf as it was when I hosted events at my club, Club Goodtimes, or Jazzi's, IV Corners, 521, C & C, and Club Heat.

A large public eye in the community is just like another member of the legislative and would represent a more diverse mix of people. A small community might be dominated in just the way Narcotic Agent Billy Bully harassed the black owned night clubs on Asher Avenue. Or dominated by those who can't afford a private attorney in court and end up with an appointed counsel who provide ineffective counsel but will get paid regardless!

The outcries from the public, ethnic, religious and interest groups allow its members to act as the majority. We elect one of our own to represent us as a whole community or district. However, no single interest group will prevail. We must stand for something or we will fall for anything. The black owned night clubs on Asher Avenue feared calling the police for assistance because it would target their very own businesses. Why are the white owned clubs in the River Market treated so differently? This is clearly and blatantly a separation of powers as we have seen within our government. Are the business owners being treated with equality? This is racism and favoritism!

To think about many politicians if given the opportunity they would resist any threats to their own power. So is Congress overstepping authority? Will our next elected president or governor be concerned for his own power? Will he exercise a veto? Will our new president or governor interfere with the administration of justice? Or will some of them continue to hook up pee-wee football players and hire their friends at the Arkansas State Parole Board. It is truly not what you know, but who you know. *"It Ain't the Whiskey"* it's called *lyfe"n"tyme and* AngieSaidThat!

Chapter 38

Dismissed Without Prejudice

Count Time

The clock struck 5:30 PM and my thoughts continued to stir. I could have been one of these prisoners without any understanding or education of our justice system. I could have been one to just take a plea or a hurricane verdict not knowing we as criminals still have rights. It never fails that many of us have made big bold prints in newspaper articles simply because of the freedom of press.

As studies show, the first priority listed of the amendments is freedom of the press. The right of the press to report and criticize the actions of the government and to be able to comment freely on public issues is essential to a democratic government.

Protection falls into two major categories, the first of which the press is generally free from prior restraint on publication. In other words, only under the rarest of circumstances can the government prevent a newspaper or magazine from publishing a story.

The government will surely respect me publishing stories of the truth within my community. My gift of writing comes from the Creator above. And my ability to express myself in areas of the constitutional laws involves the rights of criminal suspects, defendants, and prisoners. The Supreme Court rulings protect those who find themselves under arrest or in prison unjustly. One can always count on our government to get tough on crime around election time.

Here are two questions to keep in our minds:

Q. How successfully does the system balance the majority rule and minority rights?

Q. When is gender classification appropriate?

I thought about my blonde headed stud brother, B'Nutt, who loves blowing up Facebook with Q & A's. Bro, try placing these questions on your page and see what the Facebook answers are on some issue of today and tomorrow. Also, make sure you tell them AngieSaidThat. Blondie, I hope you didn't think I was just going to come to Newport Prison and go crazy. LOL

Count Time

The clock struck 6:30 PM and Sgt. Ox has gone home. I asked her nicely to sign off on my inmate check slip to mail my fourth book to my wife.

She stated. "If I sign it now, I'm going to have to keep it at my desk until they pick up the mail on Monday morning."

"Thank you!" I replied kindly and decided to keep in my care. I pressed it close to my chess as I walked off. Ugh!

"Lord, help me with these people!" She grunted.

Sgt. Ox always had something smart to say during count time. I truly liked to stay my distance from "Mrs. I'm black and that's not your hair!"

At 6:45 PM an officer yelled. "Legal mail! Richardson bring your ID." Another inmate got my attention as she was listening to the lyrics of *"Mr. Wrong"* by Mary J. Blige and Drake. *"I don't get it they fall weak to my system, but I guess I know how to pick em'. Bad boys ain't no good, good boys ain't no fun"*. The lyrics eased my mind as I read;

Received 10/04/14

In the Circuit Court of Pulaski County, Arkansas

Electronically filed October 02, 2014   Respondent

State of Arkansas   vs   Angela Richardson   CR-2013-305

Order Dismissing Rule 37 Petition

Comes now before the court the petitioners pleading and titled Rule 37 Petition in the above numbered case and the court, being well and truly advised and informed to all matters of fact and law both find:

On June 4, 2014, the petitioner was found guilty of aggravated robbery and theft of property. Petitioner appealed the conviction of July 15, 2014 and currently the appeal is still pending. Petitioner filed this instant petition on September 29, 2014.

Rule 37.2 (a) of the Arkansas rules of criminal procedures states that "if the conviction in the original case was appealed to the supreme court of appeals, then no proceedings under this rule shall be entertained by the circuit court while the appeal is pending; petitioner filed the instant petition while the appeal is still pending. Therefore, the petition shall be dismissed without prejudice.

Wherefore, the Rule 37 petition is dismissed without prejudice. It is so ordered.

Bengie Smalls,

Circuit Court Judge

Chapter 39

Playa!

This is truly another chapter in my life! After my studies in the law library, I later found out that you can only submit one appeal at a time and there is a limit on each appeal. I have always known it's better to be early than to be late, even on appeals. The reputation of this judge really made me feel some type of way. I prayed before I even read the mail. I wouldn't be surprised by this judge dismissing with prejudice everything on my case except the sentencing and the unjust time.

He should've dismissed the juror that dozed off during the trial, the credibility of the witnesses, and the juror who discussed my case with others in the hallway outside of his courtroom. I had no clue that she worked at Pulaski Technical College until she was overheard discussing it. The judge didn't dismiss the hearsay evidence either, but the judge, the prosecutor, and the ineffective appointed counsel *get paid regardless*. I realize now that they were all on the same team and working against me. It is the whiskey that most say the judge very well enjoys! Now court is dismissed without prejudice! Ugh! AngieSaidThat

I walked over to bunk 33 to fix me some lemonade as the others got ready to shower, watch movies, talk, or play dominoes. I found myself looking out the door as a handicap prisoner rolled around in a wheelchair. I very well remember in my previous book, *"The Conviction of the Gap"*, writing about the woman who killed her husband, two children, her in-laws and the dog. I finally got a chance to see her last week a few times. I watched closely as another prisoner pushed her wheelchair to the chow-hall. She had a blanket wrapped around her. She seemed very pale and weak. It's been said that she was a well-known and beautiful woman just like Mrs. Joan Rivers, may she rest in peace. She has served many years in prison and refused treatment after be diagnosed with colon cancer.

My thoughts shifted and all I could think about was one of Little Rock's beautiful news anchor named, Donna Terrell. She lost her only daughter to colon cancer in 2014. She kindly encourages our community to join a yoga class or to just exercise in general. May GOD bless us all as He continues to call his children home *now & later*.

I must say, Ms. Terrell is the only news reporter whom I want to openly share my story with about my *lyfe"n"tyme* as an inmate who has written a series of books while being sentenced to an unjust twenty-one years in prison.

As I walk around Newport Prison during my *lyfe"n"tyme,* I ask the Lord to forgive me on a daily basis. I know I'm a sinner, but GOD forgives me.

Missy looked up at me and asked. "Angie, would you like to get in the shower with me?"

"Naw, playa! I'm good and I'm in a serious relationship." I answered.

"You're in prison and she's in the free world." She stated.

"I don't care if she's in Africa, playa!" I replied.

"So, what kinda nigga are you, my nigga?" She asked.

"Well, I'm sure you were not locked up when the movie *"Roots"* came out, right? I'm that type of nigga. I'm trying to be free and understand that I can't be talked down. I'm a respectful black history type of nigga, playa. I know some of you white women enjoy plenty of us niggas behind these bars, but all I want to do is write, ma'am." I said and we both laughed out loud.

I must say Missy is really too comfortable using the term "my nigga." I know many people who get offended by the word "N" and it's a word that I will never be comfortable with. To this day most of the black gay community still ran to Jesse Road, a white gay club, where they are commonly referred to as niggers. No matter if a fight breaks out or not. The white gay club owner will not allow the blacks to grace his stage and do what they love to do, most perform in the lip-sync shows. Their talent doesn't mean anything to the white gay club owner.

The first African slaves were brought to the United States in the 1600's. By the 1700's, the slave population had grown to around 700,000 and mostly right here in the South. What about the homosexual *lyfe"n"tyme of* Bayard Rustin? He was a leading activist in the 40's, 50's, and 60's for civil rights, socialism, nonviolence and gay rights. He was the chief organizer of the 1963 March on Washington, D.C. for jobs and freedom. Why doesn't our history matter to my black gay community?

I continued to watch many commercials where Tom Cotton raised points regarding jobs and farmers. In the 1800's and 1900's farm owners' consigned former slaves and their descendants to a life little better than slavery. The economic conditions were horrendous with many blacks forced into subsistence farming or share cropping. Educational opportunities for black children beyond the basic level were essentially non-existent. Some black sharecroppers were lynched in 1908 for expressing sympathy for a black man who killed his white employer in self-defense. The justice system was biased against African

Americans and most were killed by racial motivation and others were intimidated.

Our history can't be talked down or taken away. We all must join together in our community to find ways to get the city off our backs, especially off the back of black club owners. Where are the unity programs?

There wasn't a black gay pride rally in 2014 due to my unjust incarceration. Gay Pride was scheduled to take place on July 19-21, 2014. However, in the same month, a former high school football coach with an alcohol addiction only received probation for murder. How can they say justice was served with my twenty-one year unjustified sentence?

In 1997, President Bill Clinton unveiled the president's initiative on race, which was a year-long series of events. Just like the very same things that I've done over the years for my black gay community involving studying, walking and standing up for our community with positive actions.

Most will say I am racist, but I am not by a long shot! Stanley is white, my play dad who wouldn't represent his very own indigent black daughter with a gambling addiction because she was unable to pay him $10,000.00.

My great community service deeds could've gotten me more *tyme"n"lyfe* had the jury heard what all I have done for the black gay community. My appointment of council was ineffective. Hmmm, let's see…no gun, no priors, and evidence withheld from the jurors! Is this what our state call justice?

The more I read books about our black history, laws, and American politics, the more it makes me feel some type of way. I made sure to pay attention to the elections. I had to find a way to enlighten my

American people on the things many politicians have gotten away with, issues such misusing the taxpayer's money.

"It's not fair, it's stealing!" The former governor of Arkansas recently stated about the Arkansas Highway Department. The State of Arkansas is so used to one way of thinking, the old fashioned way of things. That's probably why our highways are in such bad conditions and a change of direction needs to be headed here today!

Chapter 40

Affirmative Action

While sipping on my drink the clock struck 8:30 PM. I placed the MP4 on repeat listening to the lyrics of *"It Ain't The Whiskey"* by Gary Allan.

"With last night on my breath I stood up and said it ain't the whiskey. It ain't the cigarettes. It ain't the stuff I smoke. It's all these things I can't forget. It ain't the hard times. It's the all nights. It ain't that easy, it ain't the whiskey that's killing me. Well, I hear what you're telling me, but I got all the proof I need."

I'm so over the critics of affirmative action. The people who benefit from affirmative action are never given the opportunity to earn respect for their own actions and whatever success they do achieve is attributed to gender or skin color, instead of their talent.

Affirmative action is a term used to describe any program distinctions based on race, gender, or disability in order to promote equality. For people like me and other minorities it is harder to make it on their own, the pace is slower, but it's perhaps a surer route to success.

When I hear my black people say their careers are over, I tell them no it's not! People, we just have to have hope and make things happen for ourselves. Most folks say we can't compete, but I am living proof that yes we can! Yes, we can compete! If you can get it your head then you can get in your hand. Believe it and receive it in Jesus name! AngieSaidThat

It's not about men or women; or black or white with me. It is about being a large diverse group in my community rather than labeling us bisexual, straight, or gay. My goals have always been to increase equality in our community and other areas.

People may label me as a "prisoner" or a "felon", but I suggest you check my background and argue the facts so the truth will prevail. They can now say she is free of her gambling addiction, has booked thousands of community events, campaigned for politicians at election time, and stood strong and proud for equal rights, and has written a series of books while incarcerated in Newport Prison . They can say she's confident and focused on her vision even while facing twenty-one unjust years in prison in what many call "The Natural State". Our laws need to be reformed today regarding the *lyfe"n"tyme* of AngieSaidThat!

My movements have served my LGBT youth well, and in fact, it still shows. I'm still a role model for other disadvantage groups like black women, black studs, Latinos, Asians, gays and lesbians. Myself, as a black stud, and other gays have had a difficult struggle for success.

Even in 1992, when President Clinton tried to fulfill his campaign promise to abolish the ban on gays and lesbians in the military, he had no clue that he would touch off a national debate which caused even more gray hair in his *lyfe"n"tyme.*

Colonel Margarethe Comermayer, who after 26 years of service and was awarded a bronze star, was discharged from the Army in 1992 after acknowledging that she was a lesbian. In 1994, a federal judge ordered the army to reinstate her although the decision applied only to the pre-1993 ban on gays in the military.

Q. Are our gay rights such an issue? What about abortion? What about porn?

A. Tune in to the Broadway Joe "Who Duh Who" Early Morning Show!

Chapter 41

A Burning Fire

As the clock struck 9:15 PM, I looked up and noticed the officer in the top window looking down as I continued to research and write. I was listening to Alicia Keys & Maxwell's song, *"Fire We Make"*. The words took me again to Scott Street in Little Rock and made me think of Randi, who stands up for equality. This is the basis of the democratic form of government which allows all to participate and be recognized just as Judge Griffin, Judge Piazza, Ms. Maples and a select few who define equality in our society. In the Natural State men and women of good intentions cannot agree on what equality really means and *"It Ain't The Whiskey" folks*! Let's stay connected in this *lyfe"n"tyme*.

The thought occurred to me that same-sex marriages and religion combined together brings fuel to an already burning fire and make it hotter and hotter.

Americans say that religion is an important part of life. It is so important that Christians pay serious attention to the leaders of their churches. I could really get messy with the involvements of some of our well known bishops and preachers. It's really no different than the reality television shows with the pimping preachers. Honestly, when I get from behind these walls I will be a spiritual guidance to my youth. Today religion is more of a dividing factor than it is for us. GOD sees everything and will reveal all things. Trust me! AngieSaidThat

Chapter 42

Five More Days of Restriction...Ugh!

I stopped writing at 9:40 PM, shortly after Missy sent Stephanie over to tell me to get in the shower before 10:00 PM. I jumped up and got my soap, thermals, grease, and lotion. I was in the midst of praying powerfully and calling on Jesus as I washed the dirt off my body. I wanted to stay cleansed of it all and my body felt just as good as it looked!

The fact of no one being able to visit me due to my restrictions had me feeling some type of way. All l could think about was that I was only five days away from this petty restriction being over and getting my class back. I was blessed last night to receive a notice of approval for Kim to visit and receive phone calls. I even wrote Ms. Johnson in the visitation office to personally thank her. I also told her I respected her job and I know it must not be easy trying to be attentive to all the prisoner's complaints and processing approval forms.

I wonder as a prisoner, will our newly elected governor even consider me writing political ideology? A set of beliefs on how government and society should be organize. Even as a prisoner, it can be achieved. I know I can do whatever I set my mind to. But, will it help our prisoners and the American people make sense of this political world we are living in today? Am I keeping it too real? Some people rather have 100 pennies versus four quarters in their pocket trying to impress fake friends and family in their *lyfe"n"tyme.*

Chapter 43

Make My Body Go Boom, Boom Boom!

10:30 PM   Count Time

The officer walked in as the red light flashed to do the head count. It was Saturday night and unlike us as prisoners, those who are not trapped behind these white walls are getting red disco light ready to go to the clubs. Are they going to Jazzi's, Trois, C & C, On The Hill, IV Corners, 521, or the 50/50 club? There is currently no longer a black gay club in the city of Little Rock or the State of Arkansas.

A conversation that had just taken place reminded me of what I did not miss about my black gay club. While sitting on bunk 33 in all white at Newport Prison I was thinking about a conversation I had with Von and I stopped writing to giggle.

Von is the bunk mate to the left of me and we were discussing her girlfriend, Snap, who is also known as Keke. Snap, a stud from Little Rock, is 5'8", dark skinned, looks like a man, and has been in love twice in her short stay here at Newport Prison. Because she was *"in love"*, she foolishly stayed an additional four months past her release date. However, she is finally leaving on Monday.

"Snap started crying outside at Rec earlier." Von stated.

"Why, because she's leaving prison?" I asked.

"Well, she told me that she's afraid that she is going to cheat on me with Juicy from Memphis because Juicy said she was going to kidnap her for three days." Von answered.

"Well, is she pressing charges on Juicy? If not, she's telling you in so many words it's about to go down, Boo-Boo! Juicy is about to make her body go boom, boom, boom!" I said laughing.

"Well, she told me that Juicy knows about me. Snap is in love with me, Angie." She declared.

"Baby girl, let me tell you about my home girl, Juicy. What she wants, she gets. So what if she knows about you? She will also have you for three days too whenever you are released. You're cute enough to join the party on John Barrow, Sweetie. Juicy would love to give you some of her hunch-punch." I said laughing.

"What? I'm not going to share Snap!" She stated.

"Baby, go to bed." I said laughing and thinking Chile, if you only knew Juicy!

I tuned in listening to the lyrics of Trey Songz, *"I Gotta Go"*.

"I don't want to leave, but I gotta go right now, girl. Don't cry, you making it hard for me."

Let me tell you about Juicy. She's equal to all her lovers. She treats them all the same. She believes in fairness, equality, and surely justice. And I, AngieSaidThat, love her to death!

Chapter 44

Your Body is Your Temple

What has happened is Snap has fallen for Von, but at the same time she enjoys the bedroom boom, boom, room and overall treatment from Juicy. It's a good thing Snap and King of Avenue, both studs from Little Rock, were able to put their differences aside as far as messing around with some of the same women.

The truth of the matter is most studs get off on bragging and making statements like, "I had the baddest women in prison." King and Snap had both truly ran through these women like a freight train behind on a delivery. So did Hershey, another black stud from Little Rock. They all thought I would get involved with these prison romances and true enough I very well could have as they say, "the baddest chick behind bars" but I've been there and done that, and it didn't take a trip to prison!

The truth is I love my wife and I respect my body, mouth, fingers and my woman. My *lyfe"n"tyme* has never been based on sex.

It's not just in prison people! We as women need to respect our bodies. I can't cherish what one can't cherish herself. I have always been told that you can't turn a whore into a housewife and that's the truth. And who wants to share the same women?

The Bible defines what love should be like in a loving relationship. Love never gives up, never loses faith, is always hopeful and endures through any circumstances. I can admit to mistakes and bad decisions and even as I sit in this prison I wonder why she stays. I realize that I am unworthy of her. I miss my wife, Valerie Perry, and I know with all my heart and soul that I have turned her birthday, 12-12-12, into a nightmare. But, I am determined to turn this nightmare into a beautiful dream in my *lyfe"n"tyme*.

"Love is patient, love is kind. It does not envy. It does not boast. It is not proud." I Corinthians 13:4

I have had my share of the devil using me! I am currently enjoying my Creator and what he has done for me and blessed me with; just the same as many successful producers, coaches, lawmakers, and comedians who most talent agents are in search of. They are in need of winners! GOD never took his eyes off me, even during my gambling addiction. I allowed myself to seek the snake eyes of the dice and now I am currently in Newport Prison because of my craving to shoot dice. GOD has taken me from my weakness with an open understanding of my Bible in my *lyfe"n"tyme*.

Now that my soul, mind, and body are free of the guilt and free of my gambling addiction, I am now searching for steps to fight our justice system. I'm not alone by far as GOD has promised me he would send me the right counsel. I don't even worry about it anymore. I have faith to let go and let GOD!

All the way from the county jail at 3201 W. Roosevelt Road in Little Rock to the state prison at 302 Corrections Drive in Newport, several women have told me that GOD placed me in this place just for their purposes alone. If someone continues to belittle you and call you names such as ugly, dumb, whores or crack heads, we tend to give up on accomplishing our dreams in our *lyfe"n"tyme*. If I believed what others said about me, I wouldn't be writing my 12-12-12 series of books. Stanley, my play dad and attorney friend, told me there was no use in appealing my case. Readers at one point in my life I had more faith in this man than I did in GOD. No lie!

Everything he ever told me has been true. Later, I realized I had the money to make his attorney expertise be true. Once I got broke and unable to pay him due to my gambling addiction, he looked at me like the two sisters in *"Cinderella"* looked at her. She was dressed in rags, but GOD sent her a Prince. GOD will send me a counsel regardless if they get paid or not.

He's making a way at this moment with a small commissary ink pen and a legal pad to get the attention of our lawmakers. GOD knows I will stand for my justice and I fear no evil. I'm protected by David. It is not a mistake that I'm the only black curly blonde headed prisoner in Newport, Arkansas. In Jesus name. Amen

Chapter 45

The Blessings of My Creator

Again, I must repeat that neither the Little Rock Circuit Court nor the State of Arkansas acknowledged my great deeds in our community, but GOD never took his eyes off of me.

What also confused me during my trial is that I truly thought my community of black gays, the diverse culture, and church members would have supported me in court. Even battling a gambling addiction they knew my heart. What I know now is that none of them could ever make my dreams come true. Hey, everyone knows my giving heart, but none of them could ever bless me fruitfully like my Creator. None of them could reward me for my great community deeds or for allowing the homeless and needy to live inside my club. None of them could've taken my father's place. Stanley couldn't even protect me like my spiritual father and with him no money is required. All that my Creator requires is more of thee. He's calling me up a little higher and higher. He knew my destiny before I ever entered into this world. He knew I would face my share of so many fakes, snakes, and hypocrites!

"If you give a cup of water to one of the least of my followers, you will surely be rewarded." Matthew 10:42

My life made no sense and GOD needed me to seek his will for my life. I was too busy trying to please others and trying to get them to love me. Now, that I've gotten to know me and found my purpose in life there is peace all over me. GOD has sent me through his training program for a purpose and it doesn't take any grant money to be available to do his will. The State of Arkansas can't give me equality. My friend Dee Dee Newton often told me that it's not always a good idea to fatten a frog, because the snakes are lying low to eat the frogs. I'm done with pleasing everyone else in my *lyfe "n" tyme*.

During all of those years in the past, I didn't know which way to leap, but GOD has now spoken. He tells me to watch what I eat so that I'm able to jump higher and higher. He also tells me.

"Yes, I will see that the snakes will not be able to ever touch you again. In Jesus name."

Father, I thank you and AngieSaidThat!

Chapter 46

What's Mine Is Mine...Playa!

12:30 PM   Count Time

The guard entered as the red light flashed to do the head count. Von returned from the restroom and said smiling.

"Baaaaaby, guess what happened?"

I looked up as a white female walked over with dark hair, beautiful blue grayish eyes, and dimples. She was 5'4" and 135 lbs. She was holding a bag of cookies and handed some to Von.

"What's going on?" I asked puzzled by the smiles.

"Nothing!" They both said and smiled.

"Angie, do you want some cookies?" The white inmate asked.

"No, thank you, and what's your name?" I asked.

"Jan." She replied.

"Well, tell me what just happened before count?" I inquired smiling at her and Von. I placed my "O" magazine above my head with the charm picture of mama inserted in the middle. I also bookmarked my Bible at Psalm 23, *"The Lord Is My Shepherd"* as I patiently waited for them to answer my question. I looked over to my left at Von.

"So, tell me." I asked again.

"I just caught them trying to have sex." She stated.

"Who?" I asked.

"Jan and Mindy!" She answered grinning.

"Are you kidding me? I mimicked in my friend's, Frank Whitmore, voice.

Mindy, who is currently in a relationship with an associate of mine name B-Time, has blonde hair with dark streaks, 5'4", 140 lbs., brown eyes, and enjoys taking pills. Her father is a well-known preacher in their community near Russellville, Arkansas. She and I are not by far strangers to each other, as a matter of fact B-Time wrote her a letter last week and the first sentenced stated. "I don't care what Angie tells you."

I have nothing now or in the future to tell Mindy about B-Time, other than she needs to love herself. She has a good heart, but tries too hard to please others. I'm not surprised that she wrote that referring to me in her letter. This is a prime example of why many people need to watch out for the snakes and the fakes.

People will be in your face, but envy you at the same time. Even on Facebook you would have thought that she really loved me. There are pictures posted of us in my car together and at many of my events, but now she is putting it in Mindy's head that I have a problem with her. I found out since I have been in prison that she stopped by my wife's house after she got wind of my hurricane verdict and my unjust sentence of twenty-one years.

Readers, please know that what's mine is mine and can't be taken! No one yet has been able to take any woman of mine whom I claim to be mine. No stud or man and AngieSaidThat!

B-Time, the difference between us my friend is that I love myself and I am sure of who I am in this *lyfe"n"tyme*. My woman can't be taken and even if she leaves me in the midst of it all, it's not that she was taken, it's because she gave up on us. I would respect that and I love her enough to let her go.

I wish B-Time bountiful blessings, but the fact remains that my love is unconditional for my woman. It's called *lyfe"n"tyme!*

Tonight, Mindy and Jan enjoyed making coffee balls and shooting them up their noses to get a rush. Mindy later slept like a newborn baby that had just drunk a bottle of warm milk and had her wet pampered changed by Jan and AngieSaidThat witnessed it live in Newport Prison. This is why I don't claim friends too quickly. I will surely be careful of the ones that ride on my passenger side. I will not be too quick to say yes to the snakes. GOD has prepared me to be called to a spiritual realm. I'm spiritually going to say this to B-Time in front of my audience of readers. Someone who loves me asked me this question and due to the fact that I really do love you, let me ask you as well. "B-Time, what is your purpose in *lyfe"n"tyme?"*

Chapter 47

Watch The Flow!

As the thoughts of my wife lingered, I tuned into the song by T.I. featuring Keri Hilson, *"Got Your Back"*, and sipped a cup of water. I looked up and it was count time again as the clock struck 1:30 AM. I couldn't stop writing as I listened to the lyrics of the song. My mind raced in so many directions to escape this place, but my body laid in bunk 33 thinking about my *lyfe"n"tyme*.

The thoughts of my brother, Snoop, on my father's side, and not hearing from my family, certain friends, and even some people in the black gay community like I thought I should have really hurts. One thing I do know is anyone can love you when the sun is shining, but in the storm is where you learn who truly cares for you. I guess GOD reveals those who believe in you in the midst of your journey. The truth is I have conquered my fears and my destiny here in prison with nothing but the understanding of my *lyfe and this unjust tyme*.

This journey has proven to me that my faith in GOD is in the right place. And to think AngieSaidThat's life was just another one taken by our justice system, but GOD knows our heart, mind, spirit and soul and we have to be ready on a daily basis!

People, when I say I'm not the same, believe it! With my gifted creativity and passion for writing, my surrounding of friends and family know without a shadow of a doubt that I am talented and spiritually filled. There are no questions to be asked. I believe that my 12-12-12 series of books will make a difference with the youth in the black gay community, in relationships, to others who are incarcerated, to those who sit in judgment of others and the overall justice system.

Our State of Arkansas is so far behind and outdated with their old fashion ways of thinking and Christian beliefs. My point is that I have never claimed to be a Christian, but I am a child of GOD. I spiritually know that Jesus is my Savior. I don't need any stamp of approval from mankind. My creativity speaks for itself and my books are not by far a mistake. So, if you have a problem with it, send a text message to GOD. I'm only replying to a text from my friend Vona Cox and I am eager to find my purpose in *lyfe"n"tyme*.

May GOD bless you all from Newport Prison and in my friend, Frank Whitmore's voice, "Watch the flow in this *lyfe"n"tyme*!"

Chapter 48

Hot Socks…Ugh!

Sunday afternoon as we got ready to line up for chow, Sgt. Ox yelled. I know it's going to take y'all more than five minutes to get ready, so get up now! If you are not in line, you won't be eating! Get up now!"

The word *loud* is truly an understatement for her. Yesterday her voice was gone completely, but the volume is turned all the way back up now. Ugh!

After a long night of writing and praising GOD, I got up and brushed my teeth, washed my face, and prepared myself to walk behind the yellow line to the chow hall.

Today, the menu consisted of pork roast, green beans, pinto beans, cornbread and cake. Missy and Stephanie decided not to join us at chow, but a few days ago they made sure that I had their chicken fried steak patties. Missy wrapped the patties in tissue and placed them inside the front of her panties. I couldn't even eat the one off my plate because Officer Gupie was in the chow-hall. He's the same officer who busted me out last month in front of everyone.

"Where did you get that ice? I mean you better get rid of it Retch Now!" He screamed at me.

I had taken only one bite of my sandwich before he excused us. Not to mention, he does not care for Missy either. He's the officer who wrote her up for talking in the hallway, although it was thrown out before D.R. Court by the major. These issues are everywhere and unfair regarding "the hook-up" for certain people.

1:30 Count Time

The red light flashed as other prisoners walked in from chow. I looked around and went back to bunk 33 to write until count was over. Missy and Stephanie were bragging about me making a brave move today. I placed a big piece of my pot roast wrapped in tissue on the inside of my sock and covered it with the bottom of my thermal pants leg to bring back to the Barrack.

I came back and pulled it out like it was pork from Sim's Barbeque. I put it on some wheat bread and asked Missy to put some of the mayonnaise on it from the package that she was sharing with Stephanie.

Hunni, believe me when I tell you that will not happen again! My legs shook like a washing machine with too many clothes in it the entire time until I made a safe return back to the Barrack. This would've been another charge against me.

The case the of Pork Roast Kidnapping.

"Face the wall." The officer would demand as he placed me in handcuffs and escorted me to D.R. Court due to the given Disciplinary Report.

"How do you plea due to the fact that the evidence has been flushed down the toilet?" The D.R. Court Judge would ask.

"Not guilty, Sir! This is my first time in prison and I didn't know I couldn't take food from the chow-hall. It will never happen again." I would answer.

"I will suspend 30 days from a 60 day restriction and you are going to the hole for 10 days to think about your behavior for these charges." The D.R. Court Judge would order.

It's sad, but true. These write-ups cause many prisoners to remain locked up in prisons past their release dates. Readers allow me to share the truth about why prisons are so overcrowded. Take a look at some of the reasons for overcrowding.

You must be a Class One or Two in order to go home whenever it's time to go up in front of the parole board, but stupid D.R. write-ups occur for unknowingly accepting mailing envelopes, taking Kool-Aid, talking in the hallways, and even having an extra pair of thermals will also cause your class to be busted.

It takes months to get your class back, so you have to be on pins and needles over the smallest things. I understand that having sex, being a cutter, and cursing out the staff should be major write-ups and get your class busted down, but if it wasn't for these silly policies and petty write-ups, the beds could very well be available for those waiting in different county jails around the state with more severe crimes.

Chapter 49

We Don't Need Another Prison!

"So, I now am giving you a new commandment; love each other. Just as I have loved you, you should love each other." John 13:34

As time struck 1: 50 PM, I was getting ready to interview the life of inmate Moni, who is 5'5", 165 lb., dark skinned, glasses, short hair, really neat, cute smile with an over bite, pretty white teeth, and straight out of Detroit, Michigan.

I couldn't help but think about some of my friends that still live there, Nikky Banks, Auntie Carolyn, Tosha Banks, NaNa, and Tanya. My visits there over the years allowed me to meet and enjoy such wonderful people in my *lyfe"n"tyme.*

"Moni, how old are you?" I asked.

"Twenty-two years old." She answered.

"What area are you from in Detroit?" I asked.

"East Jefferson." She replied.

"Is that where the rapper Eminem is from?" I asked.

"No, he's from around Seven Miles." She answered.

"How did you end up in Arkansas?" I asked.

"Well, this is so hard, but do you want the truth? I haven't given it to anybody and to be open now makes me feel like I'm with a therapist." She explained and we both laughed.

"Moni, tell me the truth please. I want the dirty truth." I replied smiling.

"Well, my parents, my mom and stepdad were on drugs bad." She stated.

"Listen, I understand if this causes you to get too emotional. We can stop at any time you want to. I'm okay with it, okay?" I explained smiling with chills all over my body.

"Okay, but, I might cry later." She stated. "So, basically I was raised by my sister and brother. In the 11th grade we moved to Texarkana, Arkansas to live with my grandmother. My parents wanted to start their lives over. They wanted a new beginning in a slower pace." She explained.

"How did you end up in trouble?" I asked.

"I met a guy the same year I moved down here. He was about five or six years older than me. We met at work." She explained.

"Where did you work?" I asked.

"Pizza Hut." She answered. "It started as just a random ride home because I didn't have a car. It went from a few frequent rides home to us hanging out every day." She explained.

"Then what? I asked.

"Then things got deep and serious." She stated blinking her eyes and taking deep breaths.

"How deep?" I asked.

"He went from being one way in public to beating my ass in private." She answered.

"How did you feel the very first time he hit you?" I asked.

"I felt like he was in love with me. I wanted to experience being hit to feel loved. I know it's crazy to say that type of thing, but when it happened, I was like oh, now I know what it feels like to be loved. I know it's sad to admit it. Why would anybody want to feel that way?" She asked.

"Tell me the deep parts of your story that nobody knows but GOD." I asked.

"Well, see I was with this man for three years. My life was this man. The deepest part is the day that my mom came over to my house. I had just called her to tell her I wanted out. I wanted her to come get me, but then I called her back and told her everything was fine. She came over anyway and the next thing I heard was my mom was knocking at the door." She explained.

We were interrupted by Officer Wade who walked in to do her rounds as the clock struck 2:30 PM. I looked up at her and cut my interview off with Moni for a few minutes.

"What are y'all doing waiting for a movie to come on?" Officer Wade asked.

"No, I'm writing my book." I answered.

"Yeah, I saw you writing yesterday. Wow, Missy fixed you something to eat, huh Richardson? You came to prison to write a book?" She asked smiling.

"Looks like it." I replied. "Let me ask you something, Officer Wade. Do you feel like a prisoner with pay working here?" I asked.

"Listen, don't put my real name in that book. I will get in trouble." She stated.

"No, I wouldn't ever do that. I change all the names, okay? How long have you been working here." I asked.

"Over thirteen years." She answered. "You know we don't get raises anymore, now we just get a $500.00 bonus. But, if we don't take our classes we don't get that!" She stated.

"What do you mean by classes?" I asked.

"Like CPR, or how to deal with mentally ill prisoners, or how to shoot a gun properly, you know things of that nature." She answered.

"So, do you take your problems in here home with you?" I asked.

"No, they teach us to leave them at the door, but I do take them home sometimes and tell my husband about them. Like about the girl who cut her throat and other issues. Listen, I have a son on drugs right now. Don't get me wrong, I've done every drug there is to do, too. But it's driving me crazy. He's been to jail before and I don't know how to handle his addiction." She explained.

"Well, what if he goes to prison with the fact of you working in a prison environment. How would you feel?" I asked.

"I would be hurt because this isn't rehabilitation for drug addictions. That's why so many people return, even the mentally ill prisoners. That's what the state hospital is for, but this is the only place for them. They're building more prisons, but we need more state hospitals. There is nowhere else for the criminal mentally ill to go, but prison. The other thing that bothers me is the old people in here. Most of them need to be in the state hospital, but there is no room." She explained.

"When I first got here I remember you telling me that these women had it out for me and to stay on my bunk. Are you surprised I don't have a girlfriend in here?" I asked smiling.

"Yes, I really am surprised!" She said smiling and walking off.

This is a prime example of why our politicians should admit there is a problem. What if it's your very own son, daughter, mom, dad, judge, police, preacher, and even me, who have committed a crime due to addiction? These issues are hidden, but what is more important? They will not be able to hide it from GOD and they will still be judged by our Creator.

Be careful how you treat others. This is why I know damn well that my attorney friend, Stanley, couldn't possibly love me as his very own. Actions speak much louder than words. *People may not always tell you how they really feel about you, but they will show you.* I still love him regardless, but my heavenly father loves me unconditionally through it all. GOD will see that justice is served in Jesus name! AngieSaidThat

Chapter 50

Moni

My interview continued with Moni as the clock struck 2:55 PM in Barrack 13 at Newport Prison. As Moni set patiently flipping through a magazine I looked over at her and said. "Moni, lets continue with the interview."

"Okay!" She replied.

"What happened when your mom came and knocked at the door, do you remember?" I asked.

"Yeah, she came over and called me outside. As I shut the door behind me, she said that man is sent by the devil to destroy your life. Ain't that some deep shit, Angie? I didn't believe her, I was in love and I thought my mom was being paranoid." She stated looking me square in the face.

"When your mom told you that, what did you say back to her?" I asked.

"Nothing, she left." She replied. "I mean what can you say to that? Being raised up in a Christian home and going to church all your life. I was too far in it to believe it. It had just gone too far." She stated looking down obviously replaying it in her mind by the expression on her face.

"Diabetic snacks!" Sgt. Ox yelled. The other inmates were watching one of my favorite movies, *"The Five Heartbeats"*. It quickly took my mind back to my club at 3910 Asher Avenue. I had put on one of my AngieSaidThat events which I promoted as *"Little Rock Baddest Chicks vs Memphis Baddest Chicks"*. Kyna Love of Little Rock and Nikita Suave of Memphis, both brought out some of their city's best looking women to battle it out performing in the lip-sync show and pole dancing. Of course Little Rock won as almost 600 people packed this event out a few years ago in Little Rock, Arkansas, at my club, Club Goodtimes, the only black gay club in the state.

The love, support, and excitement was priceless! I proudly watched my former lover, DeeDee, impersonate Nicki Minaj to perfection. KeKe impersonated Trina. Zaboa impersonated Lil' Kim. Kim impersonated Janet Jackson. And Ashanti turned the show out impersonating Jennifer Hudson.

During the intermission me, B-Nutt, Jay, Andee, and Sweetz stepped out in our all black tuxedos, hot pink shirts, and black bowties and Stacy Adams shoes. We practiced for hours for two weeks straight and didn't miss one beat on the steps. We started with *New Addition* and went into *The Temptations*. I sung the lead on the song, *"My Girl"* as David Ruffin. We studied their videos and had the moves all down as if we owned the songs and labels. The night was priceless to see the unity and love between Little Rock and Memphis! Our LGBT love can't be talked down or taken away from this historical *lyfe "n" tyme* event.

I can't help but to remember the proud smile on DeeDee's mother, Lisa Cooney, face. I graced her with a special VIP table for her birthday. Even though she battled and struggled with alcohol and a drug addiction most of her life; she still had one of the best hearts ever. I enjoyed the fact that Lisa Cooney and KeKe's mom, Tiffany Lewis, who came all the way from Dallas, Texas to support her baby girl, had a wonderful time that night. KeKe's attire was on point and not to mention her mother is the baddest chick in my eyes. They always say the apple doesn't fall too far from the tree. And now I can't blame Eve from taking a bite of the forbidden fruit. Shout-out to Lisa and Tiffany from AngieSaidThat from Newport Prison!

I smiled as my mind and spirit took me outside of these white brick walls. I quickly had flashbacks about the movie and of that wonderful night, but I had to get back focused on my interview with Moni.

"Moni, tell me the deep of the deepest about what happened?" I asked.

"I went back into the house, but it was still on my mind. I set on the couch staring at him trying to see if I could see any attributes of the devil and he asked me what that was all about. I lied to him. How could I tell this man that my mom thought he was the devil? And from then on life for me got worse." She stated.

"Tell me about it." I stated while writing at the same time.

She looked up at me as her eyes got bigger and bigger. She took a deep breath and leaned over closer to me. I continued writing and trying to give her the comfort she needed to get to the deepest of the deep of her story.

"Why I am in trouble? Let's get to that part. Basically, it's so much to the story and I'm trying to put it in a nutshell. This man controlled every aspect of my life. It's like I was a puppet and he held the strings. This man no longer worked. He couldn't keep a job. I've always been independent and I had my own. He lived with me, but never helped me do a single thing. It's like I was his mom and he was a seven-year-old child. It's funny your books are called 12-12-12." She stated.

"Wow, let me make sure I put that in the book!" I said and we both laughed. "Tell me what is so deep that it is still haunting you in 2012, and also tell me about the day leading up to the crime." I asked.

"Well, I had worked an eleven hour shift two days in a row. This happened on a Sunday, the last weekend of my freedom. I spent it working to maintain while he stressed me out. Within 72 hours I got about four hours of sleep. On Friday night we got into a real bad argument over some marijuana, which he was so addicted to. I mean he had to have it. It controlled our lives. I lived in the Texas part of Texarkana and he lived in the Arkansas part. So, I set off on foot from the Arkansas side to the Texas side back to my house. He was drunk and he came after me in his car trying to get me to get in. I wouldn't get in because I knew it would have led me back to the same place that I just left." She explained.

"What place had you just left from?" I asked.

"His mom's house, then he tried to run me over with his car. I ran to the Walmart in Arkansas, so that if I needed to I could prove what really happened. I knew the surveillance cameras would be able to catch the truth of what was happening. They called the police and they came pretty quickly. The police officer asked me what happened, but I lied to them because our number one rule was not to ever put the police on each other. Why was I keeping the number one rule when he broke all the rest of them? Because I loved him and I didn't want to see him in jail. I wouldn't wish that on anyone. They questioned him and I was surprised they didn't arrest him for DUI. Instead they just let him drive off and I walked in the other direction. The funny thing is this other man, who must have been GOD, came and asked me if I needed any help or a ride to where I was going. At first I denied him, but I ended up accepting his offer. But before I could get one foot in the car door my boyfriend pulled up. The look on his face made me freeze in my tracks. My body wouldn't move. I slowly got out and close the door telling the man that it was

206

okay." She explained and demonstrated how she slowly closed the door. "I let him leave because I knew my boyfriend would have caused trouble for this innocent man. There was no limit to what my boyfriend would do." She stated.

4:00 PM Count Time

The red light flashed as the other inmates lined up to go to the chow-hall. As I returned back to bunk 33, I was in deep thoughts about the night that had caused a young lady from Michigan, Detroit life to change forever. The thoughts of Tosha, NaNa, Cynthia, Porsha, and many other women whom I knew suffered physical abuse puzzled me. Tina Turner's most amazing movie and song asked *"What's Love Got to do With it"*. The answer for some women is *"sometimes your freedom."*

Sgt. Ox entered our Barrack walking, pointing down, and counting. She walked out saying we were messy. One of the inmates commented. "That's cool, we know."

I looked over to my left and watched Moni looking in the commissary mirror as she applied chapstick on her lips and made sure her commissary eyeshadow was okay. She rubbed her hands to smooth her hair. She put on her glasses before going to chow. She had no idea I was watching her.

As the inmates returned from chow, I looked at the time as the clock struck 5:05 PM. Moni returned back to the table and we continued the interview.

"Okay, so after you got out of the car with the other man what happened?" I asked

"I started out again on foot and he kept following me telling me to get in the car." She explained.

"What is your boyfriend's name?" I asked.

"Bubba. I was five blocks from my house when I finally decided to get in the car with him. He asked me one question that should have set my journey out on foot all over again." She stated.

"What did he ask you?" I asked.

"You gone smoke a blunt with me?" She answered. "I told him no, it was three o'clock in the morning and I have been at work all day. That's when he did the unthinkable!" She stated.

Ump, Ump, Ump! I thought as I shook my head looking at Moni. "And what was the unthinkable?" I asked.

"That nigga whipped that Chevy around and took me all the way back to where I had just walked from and then told me to get out and walk from there." She stated. She pounded down on the table with her fists and screamed. "Ugh, Ugh!"

I continued to write allowing her to express her anger by banging on the table and making a number of different facial expressions.

"Then what?" I asked when she calmed down a bit.

"He dropped me off at a church and when I got out he parked and locked all the doors. He just left me standing there! So, I walked in front of the church and rolled up a blunt. I knew this was what he wanted. I gave him his fix even though I was so exhausted from fighting and working. We smoked it in the park behind the church. Then we had sex." She said quietly.

"Are you kidding me?" I asked.

She laughed and stated. "Don't judge me! "

"I'm not, I've heard worse." I replied.

"We fucked until the sun came up!" She said laughing.

"Until the early morning AM hours?" I asked looking at her laughing.

"I never made it to my house. We went back to his mother house." She stated.

"Well, how was the sex behind the church? Did it make you say Amen?" I asked as she died laughing.

"Naw, it was rough. There was no feeling. It was sex with an attitude. He fucked me dry. There was anger in it." She stated.

"Are you telling me the truth? Did he really dry fuck you, Moni?" I asked.

"Angie, I haven't told this to a soul. You are the first person I have told this to. The following day I worked another eleven hour shift. I don't know how I even survived it. But, survival is my motivation. When I got off work this particular day, I rode home with my best friend to save my boyfriend some gas. I had to give him money all the time for gas. I text him and told him I was catching a ride with her and that we were going to stop by Walmart to get her baby some Pampers and I would be home soon. But, oh no! I seriously fucked up. He called my phone cursing me out screaming. He told me to get out of the car immediately and that he was coming to get me. I continued trying to explain to him and while I was on the phone with him I saw him swerve right in front of us. He had no idea that we were right behind him. He was driving like a drunk mad man!" She explained.

5:30 PM   Count Time

Red lights flashed as we returned to our assigned bunks. Sgt. Ox entered with her pen and paper. She had a MP4 player in her hand during count time and said.

"A person tried to borrow this MP4 from another inmate. That's trafficking and trading, a major D.R.! I'm about to go home so I'm going to let them slide on this one." And then she walked out.

The red light continued to flash until count time was cleared. Moni and I walked back to the table to continue the deepest of the deep interviews.

"Do you want to continue, Moni?" I asked.

"Yes, Angie. I went to my mama's house and changed clothes. He started blowing up my home girl's phone. So, I'm like girl, let's go chill out. We went to a co-workers house to a Blunt Smoke-Out. He repeatedly called both of our phones, me and my friend's. He ran out of gas looking for me and told me that I better bring him some gas money." She explained.

"So, let me ask you this. Was he still beating you at this point?" I asked.

"Yeah." she quietly replied. "We left my co-workers house and went to her mama's house. He came over there beating on the windows and her mama said she was going to call the police. Dogs were barking as he looked in the windows and he didn't look like himself. So, I finally went out the front door. I really don't know why I even cared at this point. He told me to come with him and he drugged me to his car and I started screaming. And when my best friend and her mama came out he stopped like it never happened." She explained.

"Then what happened?" I asked.

"I ended up staying overnight with my best friend. That Sunday morning he came and picked me up. I didn't have to work so we went to his mama's house and fell asleep. When I woke up he was sleep on the couch. I wanted to go outside and smoke a blunt. I had to sneak past him to go outside on the step to smoke and text my home girl, but before I could send it, he came to the door. He hadn't shaved in days and had a very evil look in his eyes. I didn't light up the blunt because he would have wanted to smoke too." She explained.

"Did you have sex at this point?" I asked.

"No, he slammed the door and locked me out with nothing but my phone. I put the blunt inside my bra." She explained and placed her hand where she had put it. "I knocked on the door and asked him why he locked me out. He kept saying that he wanted to smoke. All I wanted to do was to go home and get the fuck away from him! He emptied everything out of my purse. All he wanted to do was to smoke a blunt!" She stated.

"Do you think he was on other drugs beside marijuana?" I asked.

"I do know he snorted cocaine and he loved to drink all the time, but I never seen him do powder in front of me, but he started pawning stuff. He couldn't have been just smoking weed though.   Anyway, he wouldn't give me back my weed, so we started boxing like straight niggas. I went to the kitchen and grabbed a small knife and he ran out the door. I chased behind him. The first stab was on the side of his hip. I didn't know that I had stabbed him until I saw red. We tussled and I stabbed him again in the lower abdomen. He fell over screaming out really loud. I snapped out of it when I saw what was in front of me." She explained.

"What was in front of you?" I asked.

"All I saw was red and anger. It seemed like everything was going in a red motion, like a slow motion. Life was like a red color!" She explained as her eyes got bigger and bigger again. "I looked down at him and said, *Nigga get up, you ain't hurt.* But he stopped moving.   I did away with the knife, until this day the investigators still can't find it. I tried to drag him to the car, but he was too heavy." She explained.

"Did you know he was dead?" I asked.

"No, he wasn't dead. I performed CPR until the ambulance got there to keep him alive. He was in my arms as I continue to perform CPR trying to keep him alive. When the ambulance got there, I called his mom and told her that they were taking Bubba to the hospital and somebody had stabbed him. I didn't tell her it was me. She told me okay, that she loved me, and she would meet me there. That was the last time she told me that she loved me. At the crime scene the police questioned me. I dropped to my knees praying to the Lord. I whispered in my boyfriend's ear, *"don't tell them it was me because I will go to jail for a really long time and I love you."* She stated crying.

"Did he answer you?" I asked.

"No, he was dying." She answered.

"Did he die at the hospital?" I asked.

She shook her head and answered. "Yes."

"What did his mama say?" I asked.

"I was at the C.I.D, Crime Investigation Department, when I called his mama, but she wasn't answering, so I called his sister's phone. She told me that Bubba was dead. We both cried hysterically." She said.

"Did they charge you right then with his murder?" I asked.

"No, I lied to them about who did it, the next day they questioned me again. One of the criminal investigators started talking about GOD. And that's when I broke down and told the truth about my abuse. They

212

wanted to find the knife but, I didn't take them to where I put it. I didn't want them to find it. They took me back to the scene, but I slipped out of my Payless shoes and out of the handcuffs. A bitch was gone!" She explained.

I dropped my commissary ink pen and placed my hand down on the table laughing just as hard as Sonta Jean, the KOKY Queen, did one Thursday night at Jazzi's after I showed her the photo from the bank footage stating it wasn't me. She laughed until saliva came out of her mouth. I walked away laughing from Moni to get me a cup of juice. I returned and looked at Moni and asked.

"Look, are you telling the truth about the Payless shoes?"

"Angie, I was 130 lbs. and this is all true. I took off running!" She explained.

I looked at her and said. "Quick on your feet, huh?"

She shook her head and said. "Hell naw, I smoked too much damn weed!"

"So, how long were you gone?" I asked.

"About 45 seconds." She replied looking at me through her glasses.

I placed my head down KMSL, killing myself laughing at her attempt to escape. I thought to myself, *you could pay more, but why?* The love of Payless shoe shoppers and she caught even more charges!

Again, folks this is *Live with AngieSaidThat* reporting the stories I have heard in my short *Lyfe "n" Tyme* at Newport Prison! UGH!

"A quick white dude on the police squad tackled me and another big 240 lbs. dude joined him once he held me down. Look, here is one of the scars on my elbow." She said and showed me her scars.

"So, what type of time are you facing?" I asked.

"I was charged with murder in the second degree and sentenced to on a half of a half with twenty years. I have to do five years and my other charges were dropped." She answered.

"Do you think his mother will ever forgive you?" I asked.

"I have had dreams where he took me to his own funeral because he knows that I wasn't trying to kill him. In the dream he sat me down on the front row at the funeral and when I looked in the casket, it was him. Sometimes, you want to know what the victim was thinking. Also, in my dreams his mother reads the Bible to me." She stated.

6:30 PM   Count Time

The red light flashed around over and over! I couldn't wait until Officer B. finished counting so I could finish listening to Moni's story.

"Moni, finished telling me about this blunt that led up to his death and your remorse over a smoke gone bad." I asked.

"Oh yeah, the blunt that I had all the way from the apartment to running from the police, to being tackled, to going to the county jail where I got strip-searched, to the second county jail where they also strip-searched me and gave me my jail uniform. The whole time I still had that same blunt in my sports bra. It remained laying on my chest through it all." She explained.

"So, what finally happened to the blunt? Did you smoke it?" I asked.

"No, I went to the last stall in the jail bathroom and got on my knees facing the toilet and I prayed to the Lord that if you get me out of this I would never smoke weed ever again in my life. This weed has destroyed my life. I repented right there on my knees. I asked the Lord to forgive me and I broke that blunt in half and flushed it. GOD allowed me to get twenty years on a half of a half and I will never smoke again. It destroyed my life and ended my boyfriend's life. The last time I smoked was July 14, 2012." She stated.

"So, overall how do you feel about lyfe "n" tyme?" I asked looking at her.

"I feel like this. If you always do what you've always done, you always get what you always got." She answered.

"Wow, that's deep, playa!" I said.

"Already! I'm glad you're impressed." She replied smiling.

"Moni, not too much impresses me, Sweetheart. Your story is amazing and GOD is amazing. He knew your heart through it all. I hate that a life had to end over a blunt, but GOD has his way with us all." I stated.

Q.   What happens when a Christian snaps?

A.   GOD has his way with us all and your heart controls your future.
     GOD is the only way, regardless of one's religion, and we should always seek him now & later. Everybody does not deserve to be in prison.
     GOD created this earth and he will seek justice for us all on judgment day. What about self-defense laws or do they only apply to the police and give them excuses to kill us?

Moni grabbed her bible for church. I looked at the time as it struck 7:20 PM. I grabbed my book and asked her to place her hands on it and pray. We both prayed together and she left for church.

Again, I thought about Tina Turner's song *"What's Love Got to do with it"*. This is what happens when a "blunt" causes "red blood".

This interview *Live with AngieSaidThat* has ended in Newport Prison at 7:15 PM on October 5, 2014.

Chapter 51

Black Gay Pride

I looked at the clock after I took my shower. 10:05 PM and the news was talking about Gay Pride in Little Rock, Arkansas. It stated that maybe two percent of the crowd was black.

I felt some type of way. People fail to realize black gay pride is all throughout our state and Little Rock is so far behind. It saddens me to know our city or state really does not care about our community needs. Instead violence and homicide continues on the rise even when someone such as myself tried to provide a safe place for us to be ourselves without judgment, but the Little Rock Narcotic Agent, Billy Bully, had me in court, stating I was a nuisance in the community. Court records in 2006 will prove this fact.

Not to mention every year and in 2011, I funded our Black Gay Pride. I invited a special guest, Jasmine Bonet, a beautiful transgender who I booked to come join Little Rock's Black Gay Pride festivities. I have great memories and beautiful pictures of her standing in front of Little Rock, Arkansas' Central High School. Jasmine Bonet acknowledged the fact that our black history can't be talked down or taken away.

What the Arkansas officials did simply wasn't enough when twelve black students tried to enter the doors of Central High school in August 1957. Public officials, including the governor blocked the doors.

The students' legal representatives went back to federal court and their case was heard in an extraordinary special session of the United States Supreme Court. The court unanimously reaffirmed the *Brown Decision* and ordered that the students be admitted. One day this nation will rise up and live out the meaning of its creed; *we hold these truths to be self-evident; that all men are created equal; August 1963*

The past eight years I've sponsored Little Rock Black Gay Pride even with my gambling addiction, but it never made the news unlike the one I saw tonight. As a matter of fact; I held it throughout the years around my birthday, July 19th. Hundreds of people joined together at 3910 Asher Avenue, cruised the Arkansas River on the Arkansas Queen Cruise Boat, and picnicked at Reservoir Park, etc... HIV/AIDS Awareness matters and is much needed in our community. It's not about race, it's about saving lives. It's the truth and a fact that our black young men are dying daily from AIDS. We can make events fun and educational and at the same time teach people to know their status and to not be afraid to be honest about their status with others before having sex.

Sure grant funding has been issued out, but I've proven facts to the Arkansas Health Department and Minority Health Department that the funds were being misused. I'm not so sure that the people issuing out the funding and the person receiving the funding weren't in cahoots together defrauding the State of Arkansas. But of course, who would believe someone without a college degree and especially now that I am in prison? However, let's be clear this scheme has been taking place long before my incarceration. I've gone as far as going to two of our elected senators' homes seeking help in exposing those using grant funding for their very own personal use. Nobody cares until it's their very own people being abused and misused. It's what I now call *Lyfe "N" Tyme*.

Chapter 52

If You Don't Stand For Something, You Will Fall For Anything

Sometimes we all have to stand for something or we will fall for anything. Justice sometimes has to be taken to the streets. Equality and fairness issues and challenges must be taken from the courts into the streets with movements for civil rights. Sometimes the movements should not only be for a change in the law, but also for a change in politics.

Little Rock just think about that good tasting Church's Chicken with a hot pepper and a strawberry drink. A combination that is sure to please even Dr. Martin Luther King, Jr., who generated pressure for change.

Dr. King declared in Montgomery, Alabama that *"the only weapon that we have sometimes is the weapon of protest"*. We all are familiar with the infamous, *"I HAVE A DREAM"* speech of Dr. Martin Luther King, Jr. It is a dream deeply rooted in the hope and desire for equality for all people.

My 12-12-12 series of books must be taken to the streets in order for me to fight for my fair share of justice in my *lyfe"n"tyme* and AngieSaidThat!

Chapter 53

Authority

On September 9, 2014, while listening to Lamont Hadley's song, *"A Change is Coming"*, I wrote the following letter to the judge.

Honorable Judge Bengie Smalls,

I, Angela Richardson, pray this letter finds you in great spirits. I can't explain to you the feeling I experienced in your courtroom on June 4, 2014, with your expertise of the law. However, I have filed an ineffective appointment of counsel Rule 37. I have been more than a great community leader and activist in our state, but that wasn't acknowledged in your courtroom. I'm sure that you can understand one's addiction of any kind.

Mr. Judge Bengie Smalls, GOD forgives us all. Equality, justice, and fairness were not served in your courtroom on June 4, 2014. This should have been a case about understanding homosexuals, but this was clearly not a jury of my peers.

GOD said to love each other us as he loves us and not judge us off Christian beliefs. Since I have been in prison, I've studied the laws and my rights. This case has proven no evidence, and presented nothing, but hearsay. I have prayed for guidance and understanding and I pray that you as a judge understand the LGBT lifestyle and our love for one another.

Respectfully submitted,

Angela Richardson

The following morning during count time at 9:30 AM, I placed the MP4 player in my ears again and listened to *"Yes"* over and over. I couldn't believe that I almost got a major D.R. last night which put me straight on my knees to pray and then to sleep early.

Sgt. High is truly one of the meanest staff members in this prison. He is a white male, black hair, thick eyebrows, 5'8", 215 lbs. and full of authority. He is always saying stuff like;

"Get away from my door. Your drawer is open. Don't come to my door asking for mail. I guess since I'm standing here I will sign your paperwork." Blah, blah, blah!

Last night after count time around 10:50 PM, I was listening to Monique Sharpen's MP4 player. As I was listening to Jamie Foxx's song, *"Slow"*, I moved my body to the beats while cleaning off bunk 33. Sgt. High had just signed off on some of my paperwork that I needed to mail off. He picked up the MP4 player while the earbuds were still in my ears. I removed them while watching him.

"So you are listening to Jamie Foxx, huh?" He asked as he turned the button off then back on again to see whose name was programmed in it.

"Here you go, Sharpen." He said and handed the MP4 player back to me while calling me by the name programmed on it.

"No, Sir. My name isn't Sharpen, it's Richardson, Sir." I stated truthfully looking him eye to eye.

"Yeah, I know. You know that's a major write-up for trafficking and trading?" He stated.

"Well sir, I didn't lie to you and I wanted to hear that song because I'm about to order my own in a few days." I replied.

Monique jumped up off her bunk over to my left pissed off and stated. "Sgt. High, I just let her see it to listen to a song."

"Well, it's the policy so, I'm taking it." He stated and walked off.

Moe punched the iron bed with her fists really hard. She really felt like I had gotten it taken by not taking it out of his hand when he handed it back to me and going along with him calling me Sharpen.

"He tried to hand it back to you!" She said pissed off at me on the slick side.

"Look, I didn't want him to take it, but he tried to hand it back to me to see if I was going to take it after he called me by the last name of Sharpen. He knows who I am. He just signed my paperwork and he very well knows who you are, too!" I stated.

Missy started talking. "He wanted her to lie and that would've been another problem. He knows who she is. Sharpen, just calm down!"

"Hell yeah, and I wasn't about to lie to him. I learned my lesson the last time with Warden Frances about some folders and an envelope." I stated.

I put my shirt on over my thermals to go talk to him. Monique walked behind me talking about she was about to fight him. I told her to calm down let me talk to him respectfully. He walked back in telling us both to sit down.

"Listen, you both know that two pieces of paper can cause your class to be dropped and a longer stay in this prison, don't you? Monique Sharpen when are you leaving?" He asked.

"In five months." She answered.

"What about you?" He asked looking at me.

"Time I win my appeal, Sir." I replied.

He held the MP4 player in his hand and said. "You both know I could write you up right now and change all that. But, I don't want to see you or anyone else here stay any longer than they have to." He stated.

Monique started crying and kicked me on my leg under the table. She was giving me a signal to try to cry or look sad so he would have mercy on us. She did "the crying" so damn good that I almost started laughing. It reminded me of years ago when my home girl, Kyna, had several outstanding warrants. The police stopped a car in which she was a passenger. She sat there pretending to be deaf! The officer continued to ask to see her ID and knocking on her window telling her to let the window down. She looked straight ahead not saying a word! (LMAO) It worked like a mug!

It took everything in me not to laugh at Monique, but it worked. He gave her back her MP4 player. He had my nerves so bad that I went to sleep unable to even write. Ugh! I promised Warden Frances that I wouldn't lie to staff after that folder incident. Not to mention if you're caught lying to staff it's a major write-up. It is just not worth it in my *lyfe"n"tyme, now & later!*

Chapter 54

Pandora's Box

I looked at the time as the clock struck 10:19 AM. I walked down to Mrs. Robbins' office. She was always fashionable and dressed classy with her black and leopard blouse, a sweater with some type of material around the collar, stone accessories, nice slacks, and always dressed to impress.

I signed in. "Hello, Mrs. Robbins." I said.

"Good morning!" She replied.

"I need my affidavit signed, please. I'm requesting a copy of my court transcript records." I stated.

She placed her notary republic signature on my paperwork, which is appreciated and very helpful to many of us behind these walls.

"Subscribe and sworn to before me, a notary public, on the 6th day of October 2014. My commission expires on 3/24/2019.

She stamped the paperwork so that I could mail it off to continue my process as I fight for justice in the State of Arkansas.

I, Angela Richardson, after first being duly sworn, do hereby swear, depose and state that: please send me a formal copy of court clerk records on June 3rd & 4th, 2014. My trial took place in Judge Bengie Smalls Courtroom. I need all recorded statements and photos shown before the court on June 3 & 4, 2014, please.

Thank you,

Angela Richardson

After returning back to Barrack 13, I placed my paperwork in the mail. It was chow time and as I headed to the chow-hall I overheard the Sergeant and other staff talking and laughing. Sgt. Marylene stated.

"Yeah, I got pregnant." They all laughed as I looked up from my paperwork

"I see you looking over here when I made that comment." Sgt. Marylene said laughing.

"Yes, I couldn't help it." I replied looking at the sergeant and we both laughed.

Sgt. Marylene is black, late 40's, short black hair, 5'6", 175 lbs., glasses, and a nice smile. She has personality and is a very good authority figure. I really enjoyed her kindness and respect for us as human beings who made some bad choices in their *lyfe "n" tyme.*

In the chow-hall, the menu consisted of beef patties, beans, sweet potatoes, a roll, and apple sauce. I prayed for us all. I drank two cups of water and asked Ms. Jackson, another favorite officer of mine to be excused, without touching the food...Ugh!

Returning to the Barrack, I put Von's MP4 player in my ear. I needed to hear *"Yes"* even after last night. I needed the gospel lyrics to grace through my body and soul.

I talked and laughed with some of the other inmates. I got into a conversation with Mindy and others not to mention I caught her and Jan myself last night on the toilet. Jan sat on top of the stall and Mindy stood in front of her with her pants unbuttoned and Jan hand inside her Pandora box making music.

I got in the shower laughing and told her to enjoy herself. The fact of B-Time thinking that I have so much to tell Mindy, which was nothing at all, was too funny. But, I do have so much to share with my readers on how to take out the time to love yourself and quit worrying about what others have to say about you, Trust me, it will make your *lyfe "n" tyme* so much more enjoyable. Mindy seem to be enjoying her *lyfe "n" tyme*! AngieSaidThat

Chapter 55

Tri GOD: Now & Later

Sometimes it's best to close one chapter in your life and start another one. It doesn't mean you don't have memories or reasons alone, but those reasons can give you what you need to go higher and higher and even closer and closer to your visions in life.

It reminds you daily of why to always keep your grass cut because snakes are lying low and looking high all around in every season. GOD will continue to allow me to believe I am a frog and I am going to continue to leap higher and higher in Jesus name. My heart is free of all of it and I will continue to pray even in prison for those who think they're free.

I might be black, I might be gay, I might be sexy to many, I might be ugly to many, I might be a criminal to many, but GOD has blessed me with an amazing gift. I'm talented and I'm amazing. Overall I'm saved and focused in my *lyfe"n"tyme.*

I looked up thinking about Snap, the stud from Little Rock, who was leaving this morning and my prayers go out to her and I hope she doesn't return. Von returned with tears in her eyes after seeing her leave. They both cried. Von expressed how she was going to miss her, but this is *lyfe"n"tyme* when you love someone in prison. The system has control of your moves. Our job in this *lyfe"n"tyme* is to stay out of trouble, people!

We all must be careful with the choices we make in life. It's so easy to get in trouble. Let's talk to our children and our troubled youth. They're our future by all means. If we can make a change in just one, the same as I did at Little Rock Job Corps, then let's do it! It's not about if I get paid or not, it's about the life of someone's child. Even my appointed counsel expressed how she needed to prepare feeding for her firstborn. I understood, not that I have children of my own, but I understand because of Elaine Richardson. My mama's *love* was so strong for us and she instilled it in me forever. I avoided growing up because I wanted to continue to live my childhood *lyfe "n" tyme* with the memories of being my mama's baby. She made things so easy for me that I was blind to her struggle with her ten children. I was blind to such thing as a father's love and help. So, no our parents couldn't pay for our college and to pick up the newspaper and see a wealthy family like the Stephens donating over $95,000.00 to Tom Cotton's campaign is unbelievable. Everyone isn't blessed or as T.I. say *"It Ain't Tricking If You Got It."*

"Yes, sometimes it takes someone such as former president Bill Clinton or President Obama to know what our communities need. Who really cares about our education? I've proven nothing except what can't be talked down or taken away. Honestly, I am the first black female lesbian in Arkansas to legally open up a black gay night club. This was something that was needed in the city Little Rock. Too many were too busy being hypocrites and judging in their church jackets, not to mention those on the down-low too busy trying to live their *lyfe "n" tyme* to please society.

GOD has made the best out of the worst situations with us all. We're not all in the position to pardon our son and his friend. I'm not a part of the pee-wee football team. If, in fact, my series of books would've been released in the midst of this election it would have been earth shattering. I never fell asleep in the midst of writing, praying, and brainstorming. How do our taxpayers feel about what has been hidden for years in our community, courtrooms, and justice systems? Can our government agree on certain Bill of Rights?

To be behind these bars unjustly and writing about the hurt, anger, pain and GOD's ways in *lyfe"n"tyme* is truly amazing. Tonight's performance briefly watching Alphonso Ribeiro (Carlton) and Whitney's great performance touched many Americans, even the other competitors. Some things can't be changed in the history of *"The Fresh Prince"*.

The *lyfe"n"tyme* took Carlton to a place within spirits that gave Americans chills, even in Newport Prison. The applause behind an excellent performance as they both ran up the steps swinging their arms from side to side. Truthfully, no feedback was needed from the judges' panel with all perfect scores of 10's held up by the judges. The judges were fair, unlike my hurricane verdict June 4, 2014.

12:30 AM   Count Time

The red flashed over and over as the guard completed the count. Briefly watching *"Dancing with the Stars"*, I stopped writing for a few seconds when the officer yelled, "Mail call!"

I received a very sweet letter from Shon Mosley updating me on what was going on in Little Rock. She mentioned in her letter that Troy Couture was trying to open up a black gay club. We mainly called him Granny because he's a little older, but he carries it well with his fashion statements. She also mentioned that the support wasn't in his favor.

GOD has truly blessed Troy with designing creativity, but he too has ignored his purpose in *lyfe"n"tyme*. We're all guilty of it at some point in *lyfe"n"tyme*. I'm truly blessed that Vona Cox loved me enough to text me and ask me what was my purpose in life! Only GOD could have placed that in her heart. People we should all *Tri GOD: Now & Later*!

Chapter 56

The Battle Is the Lord's

Let's talk about the reality of things. I've come to Newport Prison facing damn near life in prison without any priors, no gun, no evidence, and not a jury of my peers. Readers, I have truly entertained you all with *Lyfe"N" Tyme*. My goals are to help people be aware of what's hidden from all of us. It's not about me being a prisoner, which will be the biggest argument over my credibility to one's ear in order to not continue to cover up the truth.

It's time for all of us to listen to the cries behind all of the prisons in the State of Arkansas. This is not by far a mistake. Who really cares about us? GOD placed me behind these white walls for a reason. Our system has failed us and my purpose here is to expose the truth and make a difference with my *lyfe"n"tyme and* I have to thank my Creator.

"You who are young, be happy while you are young, and let your heart give you joy in the days of your youth. Follow the ways of your heart and whatever your eyes see, but know that for all the things God will bring you into judgment."
Ecclesiastes 11:9

These are the reasons why I enjoy speaking in front of many students at Little Rock Job Corps and helping our LGBT troubled youth. I started this journey shortly after I placed my addiction to rest.

I jumped in the shower and washed my back and scratched it. What's crazy is it wasn't itching, but my nails were filled with the dirt off my back. I continued to wash and scratch. I scrubbed it until there was no more dirt. I turned around and allowed the hot water to rinse the small dirt balls down the drain. I wanted to cleanse myself of it all with this small piece of the state issued soap. I wanted to leave it all behind me *now & later*.

No one will ever understand how regretful I was once I placed myself in the driver's seat on 12-12-12. I never thought in a million years that our court system would allow hearsay evidence to stand over a gap in one's teeth and sentence them to twenty-one unjust years in prison. I pray every night for the judge on my case who has a bad reputation of addictions in our community. I'm not the first, nor will I be the last to have been done wrong and sentenced unfairly.

Psalms 58:3-5
"They are born wicked sinners and hand out violence instead of justice. Does your ruler know the meaning of the word justice? "

I tuned into the song, *"The Battle Is the Lord's"* by Yolanda Adams. It's all about *Lyfe "N" Tyme*.

Afterwards from AngieSaidThat

Gayle Woods,

I pray that GOD will strengthen your mind, heart, and soul. The difference between your son, versus Denise and Nana is that they are able to visit their boys, but you have to visit a grave site. Just as the parents of Michael Brown, Trayveon Martin, and the young man in Florida whose life was taken for playing his music too loud. Also, Little Henry of North Little Rock, another young man who was gunned down by the Crispy Blue Uniforms.

Some things in *Lyfe "N" Tyme* we will probably never understand or even have closure on, however we all must stay prayed up, even behind these white walls. We all deserve justice, fairness, and equality. Those that judge will be judged themselves by the impossible. I can promise you that in Jesus name.

I love each and every one of you. I will continue to fight for my freedom. It's not that I am not trying, but the system has failed many! May your sons and many others R.I.P. They have gone far too soon from those that remind me of those purple hull peas. My Mama really showed me at an early age how to pick out the good ones from the bad ones, but I was too young to understand the rotten ones come in all forms, shapes, and sizes.

GOD bless you and I love you, Gayle!

AngieSaidThat

PS: This is why GOD led you to me. Now it makes sense after discovering my purpose in lyfe and using my gifted writing skills to share our stories. It all makes plenty of sense *now & later* in my *lyfe"n"tyme!* To GOD be the glory and just say *"Yes"*.

To the Staff of the McPherson Unit in Newport, Arkansas

Most of you look at this job the same as my court appointed counsel who handled my case with the attitude of *"I'm going to get paid regardless."* We understand it's a job, but take in consideration that every prisoner is not the same. I've seen the racism against the bi-racial couples, black studs, and disrespect towards prisoners' period! Some of you have become a prisoner with pay behind these white walls. I wonder do you look at our former Chaplin the same for breaking the law? Some of you are prejudice and show favoritism with the D.R. write-ups. I have proven facts and I know this may cause me problems, but write GOD a D.R.! Place him in the hole for thirty days, place him on restrictions with no phone calls, no visits, and no commissary. Where there is a will, there is a way! He will make it possible in the midst of it all. My visit here is not by far a mistake. He allowed it to happen and you best understand that this battle isn't mine, it's the Lord's! I tried going to the Major, Warden, and Captain, but no one would listen to me, so I dropped down on my knees. None of you could do what he's capable of doing for me. To be called ignorant and told that I have the mind of the warden youngest daughter is an insult and My GOD for the officer to state, "I'm black and that can't be your hair", is equally insulting. Honey, upgrade that bun on the back of your head! Is it even yours? And I am black! These might be your Barracks, but these are truly my books and I'm getting blessed regardless! ...LOL…. AngieSaidThat!

Missy & Stephanie, you two are truly great people and I enjoyed every moment of my *lyfe "n" tyme* with the two of you!

Amanda Brown, I pray that GOD guides you through it all. You are a beautiful person. Stay prayed up *now & later*!

Gaye Sanders, your letters and support have so much love and meaning behind them. Sometimes words can't express the feelings of the love. Thanks so much, I love you!

Gina & LeLe Chism, Pat Holloway, Shirley Martin, Gayle Woods, Denise Parker and Nana, I know some things in *lyfe "n"tyme* may not allow us to understand the loss of a child from death caused by our court system, but tell the Lord, *"Yes"* and understand that we all belong to him and whenever he's ready it's nothing we can do, but say *"Yes"*. The love of a mother is undeniable and I love you all!

GOD will deal with them all on judgment day. I'm a sinner, we are all sinners, but The Good Lord forgives us all! I'm asking you all too just believe it and receive it in Jesus name!

I pray for unity and love for us all, even as a prisoner and AngieSaidThat!

Readers,

Sometimes we go to comfort somebody who has been in trouble or who is experiencing grief because a love one has died. It hurts like hell, trust me I know. But when we leave this earth, the same as Terry Howard, our mothers, fathers, brothers, sisters, and children, we must understand GOD's way of spirit versus flesh. We are the ones who are comforted and encouraged. It's because the suffering one has focused comfort, has found something to supply his need. This is what GOD wants when we go through times of trouble. He wants to use our experiences to help others, *now & later*. I call it *lyfe"n"tyme*.

AngieSaidThat

Special Quotes from AngieSaidThat

Psalms of David 32: 3-10

"When I refused to confess my sin, I was weak and miserable and I gained all day long. Day and night your hand of discipline was heavy on me. My strength evaporated like water in the summer heat. Finally I confessed all my sins to you and stopped trying to hide them. I said myself I will confess my rebellion to the Lord and you forgave me! All my guilt is gone. Therefore let all the Godly confess there rebellion to you while there is time that they may not drown in the flood waters of judgements. For you are my hiding place; you protected me from trouble. You surround me with songs of victory. The Lord says, I will guide you along the best pathway for your life. I will advise you and watch over you. Do not be like a senseless horse or mule (out the barn) that needs a bit and bridle to keep it under control. Many sorrows come to the wicked but unfailing love surrounds those who trust the Lord."

"Mistakes, why worry about a peck in your friend's eyes if you have a log in your own?"

"We all make many mistakes but those who control their tongue can also control themselves in every way." And for this reason GOD allowed me to be numb and humble on June 4, 2014.

"The worst mistake we make is the rejection of God's purpose in Lyfe"N"Tyme."

My dear brothers and sisters, I am still not all I should be but, I am focusing all my energies on this one thing, my purpose! Forgetting the past and looking forward to what lies ahead with my AngieSaidThat 12-12-12 Series of Books.

Respectfully Submitted,

AngieSaidThat

In Jesus name.

IN THE CIRCUIT COURT OF

PULASKI COUNTY, ARKANSAS

Angela S. Richardson
Defendant/Petitioner

    vs.   CR# 13-305

State of Arkansas
Plaintiff/Respondent

<u>Rule 37 Petition for Post-Conviction</u>

<u>Amended and Extended</u>

<u>Sentenced 21 Years on June 4, 2014</u>

Petitioner's conviction and sentence was obtained in violation of the Unites States
Constitution and laws of Arkansas, specifically for the reasons stated herein. Petitioners argues she was denied effective assistant of counsel guaranteed by the Sixth Amendment, as a result of the trials counsel's multiple instances of deficient performances. Petitioner notes that Arkansas does not recognize the doctrine of cumulative error on ineffective assistance of counsel claims.

"Unjust"